"We are created for stories. We read stories, tell stories, watch stories, and live in stories. Yet we instinctively know and long for our stories to fit into something bigger, more meaningful, and more comprehensive. As we read Scripture, we can see how that longing might be fulfilled, but we don't always know how to connect our own stories to the great story of redemption that culminates with Christ. This is why I'm so thankful for David Murray's StoryChanger series. These short devotionals are wonderful guides for connecting our stories with God's larger story and helping us call others into God's great story. I gladly recommend their use in personal, family, and group prayer and devotional settings."

Chris Bruno, Global Partner for Hawaii and the Pacific Islands, Training Leaders International; author, *The Whole Story of the Bible in 16 Verses*

"David Murray's StoryChanger Devotional series is exactly what Christians are craving right now. These daily devotionals are accessible in both their content and brevity. In just a few minutes each day, readers will find comfort in the truth of the gospel and challenges in following the way of Jesus. Just because the devotionals are short doesn't mean that they won't pack a life-changing punch. This series will introduce you to the Bible in the ways that you want and provoke you in the ways that you need."

Adam Griffin, coauthor, *Family Discipleship*; Host, *The Family Discipleship Podcast*; Pastor, Eastside Community Church, Dallas, Texas

"What I appreciate most about the StoryChanger Devotional series is how accessible it is to a wide range of ages. Whether you read these books alone or with others, you'll find them to be practical, easy to follow, and helpful for applying the truths of Scripture to your everyday life. My family enjoys using the StoryChanger Devotionals for our Bible reading and discussion time. The readings prompt encouraging discussions about Scripture around our dinner table each night."

Glenna Marshall, author, *The Promise Is His Presence* and *Everyday Faithfulness*

T0244637

"We live in a world that takes pride in technological progress. And yet here we are, still a people shaped by stories—our own, those presented to us by the world, and those handed down to us by history. In the StoryChanger Devotional series David Murray has crafted brief, engaging, and accessible devotions based on the biblical text. Each volume will help us understand God's story, make sense of the world around us and, along the way, discover the transformation we need in our personal story. Slow down a while, open your Bible, and let these books prompt your ponderings about God's story and yours."

Peter Mead, Pastor, Trinity Chippenham, United Kingdom; Director, Cor Deo; blogger, BiblicalPreaching.net

"If you are looking for biblically based devotional books that are surprisingly accessible to any level of Christian maturity, you have picked the right series. The StoryChanger Devotional series is uniquely useful because David Murray wrote it. He has a special writing gift that demonstrates his skill as an expositor and his shepherding intuition as a pastor. That gift is wonderfully present in every volume, and I commend this whole series to pastors to buy in bulk and distribute to your entire congregation to study together."

Brian Croft, Executive Director, Practical Shepherding

Psalms 1–50

The StoryChanger Devotional Series

By David Murray

Exodus: Stories of Redemption and Relationship

Proverbs: Stories of Wisdom and Folly

Psalms 1-50: Stories of Praising and Proclaiming

Luke: Stories of Mission and Mercy

Philippians and Colossians: Stories of Joy and Identity

Timothy and Titus: Stories of Fear and Courage

Psalms 1–50

Stories of Praising and Proclaiming

David Murray

WHEATON, ILLINOIS

Psalms 1–50: Stories of Praising and Proclaiming

© 2024 by David Murray

Published by Crossway
   1300 Crescent Street
   Wheaton, Illinois 60187

Published in association with the literary agency of Legacy, LLC, 501 N. Orlando Avenue, Suite #313-348, Winter Park, FL 32789

Cover image and design: Jordan Singer

First printing 2024

Printed in the United States of America

Trade paperback ISBN: 978-1-4335-8109-0
epub ISBN: 978-1-4335-8112-0
PDF ISBN: 978-1-4335-8110-6

Library of Congress Cataloging-in-Publication Data

Names: Murray, David, 1966 May 28– author.
Title: Psalms 1–50 : stories of praising and proclaiming / David Murray.
Description: Wheaton, Illinois : Crossway, [2024] | Series: The storychanger devotional | Includes bibliographical references.
Identifiers: LCCN 2023038127 (print) | LCCN 2023038128 (ebook) | ISBN 9781433581090 (trade paperback) | ISBN 9781433581120 (ePub) | ISBN 9781433581106 (PDF)
Subjects: LCSH: Bible. Psalms, I–L—Commentaries. | Devotional literature.
Classification: LCC BS1430.53 .M87 2024 (print) | LCC BS1430.53 (ebook) | DDC 223/.20—dc23/eng/20231122
LC record available at https://lccn.loc.gov/2023038127
LC ebook record available at https://lccn.loc.gov/2023038128

Crossway is a publishing ministry of Good News Publishers.

CH		33	32	31	30	29	28	27	26	25	24
15	14	13	12	11	10	9	8	7	6	5	4	3	2	1

Dedicated to Chris "Uber" Raines.
My fishing guide, my treasured friend, my brother in Christ.

Contents

Introduction to the StoryChanger Devotionals

Do you want to know the Bible's Story better, but don't know how? Do you want to change your story, but don't know how? Do you want to share the Bible's Story and the way it has changed your story, but don't know how? The StoryChanger Devotional series is the answer to this triple *how*.

How can I know the Bible better? At different points in my Christian life, I've tried to use various helps to go deeper in personal Bible study, but I found commentaries were too long and technical, whereas study Bibles were too brief and not practical.

How can I change my life for the better? I knew the Bible's Story was meant to change my story but couldn't figure out how to connect God's Story with my story in a transformative way. I was stuck, static, and frustrated at my lack of change, growth, and progress.

How can I share God's Story better? I've often been embarrassed by how slow and ineffective I am at sharing God's Story one-on-one. I know God's Story relates to other people's stories and that God's Story can change others' stories for the better, but I'm reluctant to seek out opportunities and hesitant when they arise.

So how about a series of books that teach us the Bible's Story in a way that helps to change our story and equips us to tell the Story to others. Or, to put it another way, how about books that teach us God's Story in a way that changes ours and others' stories?

After writing *The StoryChanger: How God Rewrites Our Story by Inviting Us into His* as an introduction to Jesus as the transformer of our stories, I thought, "Okay, what now? That's the theory, what about the practice? That's the introduction, but what about the next chapters? Jesus is the StoryChanger, but how can his Story change my story in practical ways on a daily basis? And how do I share his life-changing Story with others?"

I looked for daily devotionals that would take me through books of the Bible in a way that explained God's Story, changed my story, and equipped me to tell God's Story to others in a life-changing way. When I couldn't find any resources that had all three elements, I thought, "I'll write some devotionals for myself to help me know God's Story, change my story, and tell the story to others."

A few weeks later COVID hit, and I decided to start sharing these devotionals with the congregation I was serving at the time. I wanted to keep them connected with God and one another through that painful period of prolonged isolation from church and from one another.

I found that, like myself, people seemed to be hungry for daily devotionals that were more than emotional. They enjoyed daily devotionals that were educational, transformational, and missional. We worked our way verse-by-verse through books of the Bible with a focus on brevity, simplicity, clarity, practicality, and shareability. The StoryChanger started changing our stories with his Story, turning us into storytellers and therefore storychangers too.

Although these devotionals will take only about five minutes a day, I'm not promising you quick fixes. No, the StoryChanger usually changes our stories little by little. But over months and years of exposure to the StoryChanger's Story, he rewrites our story, and, through us, rewrites others' stories too.

To encourage you, I invite you to join the StoryChangers community at www.thestorychanger.life. There you can sign up for the weekly StoryChangers newsletter and subscribe to the StoryChangers podcast. Let's build a community of storychangers, committed

Christians who dedicate themselves to knowing God's Story better, being changed by God's Story for the better, and sharing God's Story better. We'll meet the StoryChanger, have our stories changed, and become storychangers. I look forward to meeting you there and together changing stories with God's Story.[1]

---

1 Some of this content originally appeared on *The Living the Bible podcast*, which has since been replaced by *The StoryChanger podcast*, https://podcasts.apple.com/us /podcast/the-storychanger/id1581826891.

Introduction to *Psalms 1–50: Stories of Praising and Proclaiming*

God designed us with a desire to praise him as a vital part of the human story and of human flourishing. Sadly, sin chilled that desire so that we drift toward cold formality, misdirected that desire so that we praise lesser things, and perverted that desire so that we now prefer criticizing to praising.

God therefore gave us the book of Psalms (*psalms* means "praises") to rekindle our desire to praise him, to direct our praises to him, and to give us enjoyment in praising him.

But the Psalms are for more than praising; they are also for proclaiming and predicting. They change our story of praising but also proclaim and predict the story of Christ and his kingdom. As we sing these songs, we sing not only *to* Christ but *about* Christ and *with* Christ. (Have you ever considered that we use the same hymnbook Jesus used when he was on earth?)

May these story-songs of praising and predicting change our stories so that praising God becomes part of our happy present and eternal joy.

Rich soil produces rich fruit.

1

The Great Divide

How can I be happy? This is the most frequently asked question in the world. It's no wonder that the book of Psalms begins with "Blessed is the man."

Blessed means more than happy. It means accepted and approved by God. If God says, "You are blessed," he's saying, "I'm smiling upon you." Surely nothing could make us happier than knowing that God is happy with us. How does God's happiness *with* us come *to* us? Psalm 1 describes four channels of blessing.

God Gives Happy Friendships 1:1

"Blessed is the man who walks not in the counsel of the wicked, nor stands in the way of sinners, nor sits in the seat of scoffers" (1:1).

Some friendships are fatal. The person who walks with the wicked will soon stand with the wicked and eventually scoff with the wicked. Such friendships bring God's curse upon us.

Some friendships are flourishing. While wicked friendships are fatal to happiness, good friendships fertilize happiness. If we walk in the counsel of the godly, follow the ways of the godly, and join in godly praise and encouragement of good, then we will be truly blessed.

Bad buddies result in sad souls.

"Happy friendships are great, but where do I get happy feelings?"
True happiness springs from true words.

7

God Gives Happy Words 1:2

"His delight is in the law of the LORD, and on his law he meditates day and night" (1:2).

Godly people delight in the truth. "The law of the LORD" is not just the Ten Commandments; it refers to the whole of God's teaching. Believers don't just read the Bible; they enjoy the Bible. It's a pleasure to them. It excites them. They love to think upon it throughout the day and night. *Godly people meditate on the truth.* The Hebrew word that we translate as *meditating* means chewing or sucking. Think of how we savor our favorite candy. We take our time and try to relish every last atom of flavor. The Bible's words don't just pass through our eyes or ears; we grab them and feast upon them.

When we delight in God's word, we meditate on it. When the word makes us happy, we want to meditate more. It's a blessed circle.

Good facts bring good feelings.

"What do happy feelings produce?"
Look at the believer's branches.

God Gives Happy Fruit 1:3

"He is like a tree planted by streams of water that yields its fruit in its season, and its leaf does not wither. In all that he does, he prospers" (1:3).

A fruitful tree is planted near water, bears fruit, and is evergreen. This idyllic scene is a beautiful sight to God and others. This kind of person prospers in all that he or she does. This verse is referring not to financial prosperity but to spiritual prosperity.

Rich soil produces rich fruit.

"That makes me happy now, but will I be happy in the future?"
Let's look ahead.

God Gives Happy Hope 1:4–6

Those who live without God will be cursed (1:4–5). They have no happy fruit or future. They are like chaff, useless and worthless to God and therefore rejected by God. They are excluded from the congregation of God's people now and forever.

Those who follow God's formula for happiness will be happy forever. They will stand in the congregation of the righteous because Christ has made them righteous (1:6).

Our blessed present is a taste of our blessed future.

Changing Our Story with God's Story

Although we use this psalm to praise God for any blessed happiness in our lives, we use it, above all, to worship Jesus, the ultimate blessed man. Jesus loved his friends so much that he laid down his life for them (John 15:13). He loved the word of God, was a fruitful evergreen tree, and had certain hope of future joy (Heb. 12:2).

Summary: How can I be happy? *Discover and deepen happiness in God's family, book, fruit, and home.*

Question: How will this psalm change your pursuit of happiness?

Prayer: Blessed Savior, I worship you as the ultimate happy man. Please share your happiness with me and through me.

Christ offers peace to those who offer war.

2

The First World War

Do you ever feel frightened by the violent and virulent opposition to Christ and to Christians that surrounds and threatens us today? I do. But I'm more scared for my children than for myself. If it's like this now, what will it be like for them in ten years' or twenty years' time? How do we find peace during the world's war against Christians? *How do we fight fear of faith's foes?*

When fear of faith's foes floods my heart, I turn to Psalm 2, and there I find the calming confidence of Christ.

The Lord Has Multiple Enemies 2:1–3

The Lord has innumerable enemies. The nations rage against him (2:1a). The peoples plot against him (1b). The kings stand against him (2:2a). The rulers conspire against him (2:2b).

However diverse these enemies, their one united aim is to destroy God's rule. They unite together against the Lord and against his anointed. If we were to spy on their plotting, we would hear them say, "Let us burst their bonds apart and cast away their cords from us" (2:3).

Christ has multiple enemies,
but they all have one united aim.

"Now I'm more scared than ever. I thought we came to Psalm 2 for calm confidence?" Here it comes.

The Lord Will Defeat His Enemies 2:4-9

- The Lord *sits* in the midst of the chaos—unruffled, unstressed, unworried, and in total control (2:4)
- The Lord *scoffs* because he is secure and victorious, like a Dad holding a little angry boy at arm's length (2:4).
- The Lord *speaks*. A scroll is unrolled, announcing the worldwide extent of the Lord's rule (2:5-8)
- The Lord *smashes*. Before battle, ancient rulers would call a potter to make a model of the city about to be attacked. The king would then bring his scepter down upon it to show what was about to happen to his opponents (2:9). This vivid graphic warning could persuade hostile enemies to lay down their arms.

If we laugh long at God, God will laugh last at us.

"So, what do we do about our enemies in the meantime?"
Offer them peace.

The Lord Offers Peace to His Enemies 2:10-12

Despite their violent opposition and their ultimate defeat, God's enemies can still choose peace. In the closing words of this psalm, God calls his enemies to be wise citizens (2:10), reverent servants (2:11), and happy refuge-takers (2:12c).

Our fight song is therefore also a giving-of-life song. We invite our enemies to a kiss of life. "Kiss the Son, lest he be angry, and you perish in the way, for his wrath is quickly kindled. Blessed are all who take refuge in him" (2:12).

We find many types of kisses in the Bible: greeting (Gen. 33:4), acceptance (Luke 15:20), allegiance (1 Sam. 10:1), adoration (1 Kings 19:18), and affection (Luke 7:45). All these are included in a kiss to the Son of God.

Christ offers peace to those who offer war.

Changing Our Story with God's Story

The New Testament tells us that this psalm is a direct and clear prophecy of Jesus Christ, whose very name is Jesus Anointed (Matt. 3:17; 17:5; Acts 4:25–27; 13:33; Rom. 1:4; Heb. 1:5; 5:5). We therefore use these verses to kindle love and worship for him. Jesus is the Lord's Anointed (Ps. 2:2), King (2:6), Son (2:7), Judge (2:8–9), and Savior (2:10–12). As we turn from our enemies to Christ, we find our frothing fears replaced by his calm confidence. His seat, his scoff, his scroll, and his scepter are our greatest comfort. This is our fight song.

Summary: How do we fight fear of Christ's foes? *In the face of hostility and persecution, find calm confidence in Christ and continue to offer Christ's peace to even his worst enemies.*

Question: What comforts you most? The Lord's seat, scoffing, scroll, or scepter?

Prayer: Anointed King, comfort me with your laugh at your enemies and challenge me to offer your love to your enemies.

Peace nourishes praise and praise nourishes peace.

Hear
God's Story

Change
Your Story

Tell
the Story

Change
Others' Stories

3

Moving from Panic to Peace

PSALM 3

I've had panic attacks a few times in my life, usually after times of prolonged stress. The first time it happened I was sure I was dying, and I went to the emergency room. It can be embarrassing to walk into the ER announcing, "I'm having a heart attack!" and to walk out with a nurse saying, "It's just stress."

Since then, I've had other panic attacks, but, having learned the difference between lesser problems like panic attacks and far more serious problems like heart attacks, I save myself the embarrassment (and the expense) by pausing and praying until peace returns. *How do we pray ourselves from panic to peace?*

In Psalm 3, David provides us with a pattern prayer that shows us how to move from panic to prayer to peace to praise.

When Christians Feel Panic, They Pray 3:1–4

David's enemies were many and murderous, so much so that he cried out, "O Lord, how many are my foes! Many are rising against me; many are saying of my soul, 'There is no salvation for him in God'" (3:1–2).

When David saw how many enemies he was facing and heard their plans to destroy him, alarm, horror, and dread gripped him. He felt the external pressure of his terrifying enemies and the internal squeeze of his terrified emotions.

He panicked, but he also prayed. He brought his panic to God. He didn't hide it, try to minimize it, or put a brave face on it. No, this courageous warrior was vulnerable and transparent before God and others. Then, having laid bare his raw feelings of weakness and fear, he reminded himself of the character of the God to whom he was praying: "But you, O LORD, are a shield about me, my glory, and the lifter of my head" (3:3).

No matter how many enemies David had and how many attacks they made on him, God's shield was wider and thicker. Fear was replaced with sight of the glory of God. Instead of walking about downcast, David could lift his head high knowing God had answered his panicky prayer (3:4).

Panic should lead to prayer not despair.

What happens when God answers our prayer?
Peace and praise.

When Christians Get Peace, They Praise 3:5-8

What happened when David prayed? Instead of panic consuming him, peace overwhelmed him: "I lay down and slept; I woke again, for the LORD sustained me" (3:5).

The Lord removed paralyzing fear and replaced it with refreshing sleep. God's provision of sleep was part of his answer to David's panic. It changed his perspective and psychology. When he opened his eyes, his enemies were still there, but his fears had diminished, even vanished: "I will not be afraid of many thousands of people who have set themselves against me all around" (3:6). Instead of looking ahead and seeing darkness and death, he now saw hope and a future.

Earlier, his enemies had claimed that there was no salvation for David, and David seemed to agree. But now he prays for salvation with confidence: "Arise, O LORD! Save me, O my God! For you strike all my enemies on the cheek; you break the teeth of the wicked" (3:7).

Full of panic before, David is now full of prayer. Full of peace, he is now also full of praise: "Salvation belongs to the LORD; your blessing be on your people!" (3:8). He praises God for his sovereign salvation and the blessing of peace.

Peace nourishes praise and
praise nourishes peace.

Changing Our Story with God's Story

This psalm of David is also a psalm of Christ. Jesus experienced the ups and downs of this psalm (Heb 5:7). He had to battle against anxiety and panic, and he did so with prayer that brought him peace and made him praise. When we panic, Christ is our peace and our praise.

Summary: How do we pray ourselves from panic to peace? *Use prayer to change panic into praise-filled peace.*

Question: What causes you to panic, and how will you use this psalm to replace panic with peace?

Prayer: My Vulnerable Savior, help me to be vulnerable about my weaknesses so that I can be strengthened by prayer, peace, and praise. Amen.

God gave thousands of promises for our thousands of doubts.

4

Simple Evangelism

PSALM 4

We all love to love. In one way or another, we all want more love in our lives. A husband asks, "How can I love my wife more?" A mother asks, "How can I love my children more?" The Christian asks, "How can I love God more?" or "How can I love the Bible and God's people more?" Or, less frequently, *"How can I better love my neighbor?"* We need to ask ourselves that question because Jesus said neighbor-love is the second most important of all loves (Mark 12:31). That's the question Psalm 4 helps us answer.

We Love Our Neighbors by Praying for Them 4:1–2

David was in deep and distressing pain, causing him to cry out to God for relief (4:1). The sinful lifestyles of the ungodly were crushing him (4:2). God had been working in David, showing him the need of the ungodly and filling him with painful concern for them.

David brought this debilitating pain to God because God had graciously heard his prayer for relief before. He therefore called upon God again to hear and answer by relieving David's godly soul-pain for the ungodly's soul-condition. Soul-pain that's rooted in soul-care is healthy pain. It's a sign of life. But when it is too much or for too many or goes on too long, it can become unbearable.

Some soul-pain is a sign of soul-life.

"What happens when God answers our prayer?"
We start pleading with our neighbors.

We Love Our Neighbors by Pleading with Them 4:2–5

Having appealed to God, David then appeals to sinners. He shares with them God's perspective on their sin, the Christian's status, and Christ's sacrifice.

David pleads with them about their *sordid sin* (4:2). Speaking as God's spokesman, David tells his neighbors what God thinks about sin and how he views their lives. He tells them sin is shameful, sin is pointless, sin is a lie, and sin is against God.

David pleads with them about the Christian's *special status* (4:3). He urges these suffering sinners to consider the status and honor that believers have. They have been specially selected by God for the special favor of being God's special property that he takes special care of.

David pleads with them about Christ's *special sacrifice* (4:5). Knowing that God blessed the Old Testament sacrifices to bring people to faith in the coming Messiah, he pleads with them to think about them (4:4) and offer them (4:5).

Appeal to God for sinners so that you can appeal to sinners for God.

"How can we encourage our neighbors to seek godly status and not sin?" We highlight gospel promises.

We Love Our Neighbors with Gospel Promises 4:5–8

We encourage our neighbors toward the gospel with the promises of the gospel.

God promises spiritual *protection* (4:5). Christ's sacrifice turns away God's anger like an umbrella turns away the rain from our heads.

God promises spiritual *pleasure* (4:6–7). People are seeking pleasure. The psalmist tells us to find it in God.

God promises spiritual *peace* (4:8). Whether I wake up in this world or the next, I have total peace. I trust God as much as I trust my bed. He's a perfectly comfortable place for my soul.

God gave thousands of promises
for our thousands of doubts.

Changing Our Story with God's Story

Praise God that he sent prayerful evangelists into our lives, men and women who appealed to God for our souls and then appealed to us for our souls. They bravely pointed out our sins and lovingly pointed us to faith in Christ's sacrifice, and by grace we entered into a life worth living and a death worth dying. Praise God for the gospel and for evangelists.

Summary: How can I love my neighbor better? *Love your neighbor better by sharing the gospel better.*

Question: How will you show love to your neighbors?

Prayer: Loving Savior, thank you for loving me with the gospel. Help me to love my neighbor with the gospel.

God's love is a fortress more than a feeling.

Hear
God's Story

Change
Your Story

Tell
the Story

Change
Others' Stories

5

Holy Hatred
and Holy Love

PSALM 5

Most hate is not holy and therefore should be repented of. But some hate is holy, and can even be part of our praise to God.

If we're honest, we all feel hate at times. We all feel guilty about it at times, and we know it's harming us. So, *how should we hate in a healthy way?* How can we process hate in a way that helps us rip out sinful hate and ripen healthy hate?

Psalm 5 demonstrates the validity and value of holy hate. Like many psalms, it doesn't progress in a straight line from A to Z, but moves back and forth from God's love (5:1–3) to God's hate (5:4–6), to God's love (5:7–8) to God's hate (5:9–10), and then to God's love again (5:11–12).

God Hates Evil Workers   5:4–6, 9–10

God loves all people because they are made in his image, and he is our model for loving even our enemies (Matt. 5:43–48). We are to love them for the same reasons that God loves them: he made them in his image. We are to love them in ways that reflect how God loves them: through prayer, provision, protection, politeness, and preaching the gospel.

But God also hates evil people for destroying his image (5:4–6). That means sometimes God hates those he also loves. Is this a contradiction? No, because God loves evil people in some ways, but hates evil people in other ways. He loves them because they are image bearers, but hates them as evil people destroying his image. As this psalm puts it, God does not delight in the wicked (5:4a); he does not dwell with them (5:4b–5a); he hates all evildoers (5b); he destroys liars (5:6a); he abhors murderers and deceivers (6b, 9); and God will judge evildoers (5:10).

Love for God requires hate
for the opposite of God.

"So, how does God feel toward me?"
If you're a believer, God loves you.

God Loves His Good Work 5:7–8, 11–12

"But I, through the abundance of your steadfast love, will enter your house. I will bow down toward your holy temple in the fear of you. Lead me, O Lord, in your righteousness because of my enemies; make your way straight before me" (5:7–8).

David knows that holy hatred is potentially dangerous and therefore he returns again and again to luxuriate in God's luxurious love. Hate comes easy, so it needs to be fueled with God's flaming love. Look at all that flows from God's love: it changes us into worshipers (5:7), helps us live godly lives (5:8), gives us joy (5:11), and protects us (5:11).

"But let all who take refuge in you rejoice; let them ever sing for joy, and spread your protection over them, that those who love your name may exult in you. For you bless the righteous, O Lord; you cover him with favor as with a shield" (5:11–12).

God's love for David inspires love for God in David. As God's love is poured into his heart, David responds in love. What a joy it is when God's love for us initiates our love for God. It lifts us up, and we lift God up. It's no wonder that David can end the psalm by rejoicing that God's love is his refuge, protection, and shield.

God's love is a fortress
more than a feeling.

Changing Our Story with God's Story

God's holy hatred and God's holy love shield us in the midst of our enemies' hatred and hostility. Let's use these to fend off not just our enemies' hatred but our own unholy hatred. Instead let's love and rejoice in God's perfect hatred and perfect love, as David did imperfectly and the greatest Son of David did perfectly (Heb. 1:9).

Summary: How should we hate in a healthy way? *We let our enemies' hatred drive us to God's holy hatred and holy love for double protection and double comfort.*

Question: In what ways did Jesus fulfill this psalm and therefore model how we can live it?

Prayer: Holy God, help me to hate what you hate by being loved by you and by loving what you love.

Letting our feelings out lets God's healing in.

Hear
God's Story

Change
Your Story

Tell
the Story

Change
Others' Stories

6

Praising by Lamenting

PSALM 6

Jason was suffering on all fronts. His psoriasis felt like a thousand mosquito bites. His family was divided over whether to call their transgender son by his new name or her old name. Jason's church felt like a war zone, with casualties on both sides. He'd lost his job a few months back, and was deeply in debt. He was almost insane with insomnia. Yet, when people asked him how he was doing, "Mustn't complain" was his auto-response. He'd heard this many times from his father, who shared the belief that all complaining was dishonoring to God.

Jason's wife, Julia, had watched helplessly for months; he wouldn't talk to her or anybody else about how he was really doing. She feared an explosion was brewing because he continued to bottle everything up. One day, though, she came across Psalm 6, and noticed that David did not bottle things up but brought his problems to God in a praise-filled lament. She shared it with Jason that evening and asked him to study it with her. *"How can you praise by lamenting?"* he murmured as they began to read it together.

God Wants to Hear Our Laments 6:1–7

In this psalm, David took the facts and his feelings to God. He didn't just coldly and mechanically list the facts. Neither did he uncontrollably vent his feelings. No, he took both the facts and his feelings. He described what he was suffering and how he felt about it.

He described spiritual sufferings (6:1), bodily sufferings (6:2), psychological sufferings (6:3), and social sufferings (6:7). But he did so with feeling throughout the first part of the psalm: I'm scared (6:1); I'm depressed (6:2); I'm sore (6:2); I'm troubled (6:3); I'm impatient (6:3); I'm dying (6:4–5); I'm tired (6:6); I'm moaning (6:6); I'm crying (6:6); I'm weakening (6:7).

Lots of facts and lots of feelings. The facts controlled his feelings, and his feelings intensified the facts.

Lament to God, not about God.

"But what good does this do?"
When we come with laments, God comes with healing.

God Wants to Heal Our Laments 6:8–10

What happens when we take the facts and our feelings to God? First, David has new confidence: "The LORD has heard the sound of my weeping. The LORD has heard my plea; the LORD accepts my prayer" (6:8–9). Having brought the facts and his feelings to God, David enjoys new faith. Facts + Feelings = Faith. His mood is very different, as is his attitude toward God and himself.

Second, David has new hope. "All my enemies shall be ashamed and greatly troubled; they shall turn back and be put to shame in a moment" (6:10). Facts + Feelings = Faith. This doesn't mean that God immediately healed David's sufferings. It means that David had real hope that God would eventually heal his sufferings. They wouldn't go on forever. And that hope is itself a super-healer.

Letting our feelings out lets God's healing in.

Changing Our Story with God's Story

As Jason let this psalm sink in over the next few weeks, he realized that God wanted him to come to him with all the facts and all his feelings about his problems. When we bring our complaints to God in the form of lament, our complaints can be turned into praising. God is honored and exalted when we cry to him about the facts and our feelings, and when we walk away with new hope and confidence. Godly complaining should end with godly confidence.

Psalm 6 also gave Jason new insight into the life of Christ as he thought of Christ's perfect complaint and perfect confidence even at his lowest point (Matt. 27:46). At no point did he doubt the final outcome of his sufferings and sighs.

Jason began to think more about eternity. This psalm will be fulfilled by Christ in the new heavens and new earth. He will heal all our complaints forever, and his enemies' never-ending complaints will commence.

Summary: How can you praise by lamenting? *Lift up your complaints using fact- and feeling-filled laments, and you'll lift up God and yourself.*

Question: How will you turn your complaints into praises?

Prayer: Compassionate Creator, help me to bring you my complaints as praises and walk away with confident praises. Amen.

Perfect justice results in perfect praise.

7

"Enemies? I Have No Enemies"

PSALM 7

Have you ever been the victim of injustice? It's agony, isn't it? It makes you feel so frustrated, angry, so vengeful, and depressed.

What is injustice? It's being punished for something you didn't do, or getting off when you should be punished. Injustice is having a loved one murdered, but the murderer is never found, or never found guilty, or sentenced to just a few years in prison. It's being bullied at school, but the school tells you to "just suck it up." It's being slandered, misrepresented, or defamed behind your back or online. It's being targeted by the devil, the most unjust being in the universe.

When we lose justice, we can lose our peace, our joy, our relationships, our health, and our lives. *How can we respond to injustice so that we gain more than we lose?* Let's ask King David, because he experienced injustice at the hands of his brothers, King Saul, Ahithophel, Shimei, his son Absalom, and many others.

God Is Just in Saving the Innocent 7:1–10

Save me, because I can't save myself (7:1–2). David knew that his enemies were too many and too malicious. They were too large and too lion-like. They wanted to rip his body and rend his soul. They were savages—but God was his refuge and protection.

Save me, because I am innocent (7:3–5, 8). David knew that, before God, he was guilty and unrighteous. But, compared to his enemies, he was just and innocent. Also, he could rightly plead innocence regarding the specific slanders, charges, and accusations they were leveling against him. Indeed, he could boldly pray, "If I've done what they accuse me of, then let me be punished and even damned."

Save me, because your people are discouraged (7:6–7, 9–10). David's unjust sufferings had sown doubts about God's justice among the people of God. Their faith was failing and their worship weakening. David pleads with God to awaken his justice to reawaken their worship (7:6–7).

If David could sing this, how much more could Jesus, the greatest-ever victim of injustice. This psalm was written by David for the greatest Son of David.

Injustice brings us to Jesus and Jesus to us.

"But what about the unjust?"
They won't get away with it forever.

God Is Just in Punishing the Unjust 7:11–17

God is preparing judgment for the wicked (7:11–13). Not a day goes by without God feeling indignant about injustice (7:11). He is sharpening his sword and setting arrows in his bent bow, ready to fire death into the unjust (7:12–13). David turns away from what he is suffering to what his enemies will suffer forever.

The unjust are preparing judgment for themselves (7:14–16). Although the wicked spend their days conceiving evil, pregnant with evil, and giving birth to evil, their evil will one day turn against them and crush their skulls, the headquarters of their evil (7:14, 16).

God is preparing praise for himself (7:17). This psalm of lament about injustice turns into a psalm of praise for God's justice. The greater the injustice, the greater the praise when justice is finally accomplished (Rev. 19:1–5).

Perfect justice results in perfect praise.

Changing Our Story with God's Story

The best way to sing Psalm 7 is to think of our greatest enemy, the devil. Although we cannot see him, he is totally committed to the destruction of every Christian everywhere. Reread and resing this psalm with him in mind, and you'll soon find your heart engaged and your volume increased. Worshipfully ask God to save you and all his people from worldwide enemies, cultural enemies, and our greatest spiritual enemy, the devil.

Summary: How can we respond to injustice so that we gain more than I lose? *Use God's justice as a refuge and shield to gain God and glory.*

Question: How will this psalm change your attitude toward victims and perpetrators of injustice?

Prayer: Just God, be my refuge and shield when I suffer injustice so that whatever else I might lose, I gain you and you gain glory.

God's children are stronger than the devil's battalions.

8

The Strongest
Uses the Weakest

PSALM 8

Research suggests that the experience of awe can make us happier, healthier, more humble, and more connected to the people around us.[1]

What is awe? The scientific definition is, "The emotion we feel in response to something vast that defies our existing frame of reference in one area or another, and leads us to change our perception of that frame of reference." More simply, "Awe makes us feel small."[2] Or, even more simply: it's the chills.

Awe makes us feel small in the presence of something much bigger than us. It's not a feeling that humiliates or demeans us; rather, it's a sense of littleness that helps us thrive and flourish. *So, how do we get awe?* David teaches us how in Psalm 8.

Develop Awe by Looking at Our Humanity

We develop awe not simply by looking at ourselves, but by looking at ourselves compared to the universe. Awe comes to us not when we think we are so big and strong, but when we realize we are small and weak.

God uses weak humanity to win his wars (8:1–2). In the first line of this praise song, David praises God as the ultimate and almighty Creator

---

1 Summer Allen, "Eight Reasons Why Awe Makes Your Life Better," *Greater Good Magazine*, September 26, 2018, https://greatergood.berkeley.edu/.

2 Sarah DiGiulio, "Why Scientists Say Experiencing Awe Can Help You Live Your Best Life," *NBC News*, February 19, 2019, https://www.nbcnews.com.

whose name is excellent throughout the earth and whose glory is displayed in the heavens (8:1). The second line introduces a striking contrast, as David sings of babies' and infants' mouths. What could be smaller or weaker? And yet God uses small and weak humanity to defeat his violent and vicious enemies (8:2). God strengthens the weak to silence his enemies.

God uses weak humanity to manage his world (8:3–9). In the second part of the song, David again contrasts the mighty with the small, this time comparing the vast creation with the small creature called man (8:3–4). Just as God uses weak humanity to win his wars, so he uses weak humanity to manage his world (8:4–8). God thinks about us (8:4a), cares for us (8:4b), lifts us up, and crowns us with glory and honor by giving us power over all creation (8:5–8).

God's children are stronger than the devil's battalions.

"But we don't see this psalm perfectly fulfilled yet."
No, not in humanity—but yes in Christ.

Develop Awe by Looking at Christ's Humanity

Humanity fulfills this psalm in a limited and imperfect way. But, as Hebrews 2:8 reminds us, Jesus fulfilled this psalm perfectly in his humanity.

God used Christ to win his wars (8:1–2). We praise God for Christ who, by becoming weak in his incarnation, won God's wars. Christ thought upon weak humanity, visited weak humanity, and even took on weak humanity himself. He became a little lower than the angels to defeat God's enemies. What awesome grace!

God uses Christ's humanity to manage his world (8:3–9). Because Christ wins God's wars, he now manages God's world (Matt. 28:18–20; Phil. 2:6–11). He was made a little lower than the angels for a short time and then crowned with glory and honor by being given all authority in heaven and on earth. We see this not with our physical eyes but with our spiritual eyes. What awesome glory!

Because God is awesome,
we are full of awe.

Changing Our Story with God's Story

Be in awe of how God used Christ's weak humanity to advance his providential and saving purposes. Next time you look at yourself, remember that Jesus took on flesh to defeat his and your enemies. Next time you look at the stars, the moon, or the sun, remember that God has placed his Son on a throne above them all. Through him, the Lord's name is excellent in all the earth.

Summary: How do we get awe? *We use our humanity and Christ's perfect humanity to increase awe of God.*

Question: Give examples in the Bible and in your life of how God uses the weak to defeat the strong.

Prayer: Awesome God, continue to amaze me as I see how great you are and how small you became to save me from my sin.

God judges the wicked out of love for his people.

9

Two Reasons to Celebrate God's Judgment

PSALM 9

Safety-ism is "a culture or belief system in which safety (including emotional safety) has become a sacred value that makes people unwilling to balance other practical and moral concerns."[1] So write Greg Lukianoff and Jonathan Haidt in their bestselling book, *The Coddling of the American Mind: How Good Intentions and Bad Ideas Are Setting Up a Generation for Failure*. They argue that embracing the culture of safety-ism, with its trigger warnings and safe places, has interfered with young people's social, emotional, and intellectual development.

Opponents of safety-ism are not opposed to safety or to taking sensible safety precautions. They are opposed to safety being the only value in all considerations. They are opposed to some of the methods that safety-ism promotes. And they believe it makes people less safe in the long run.

As Christians we would also argue that safety-ism excludes the most fundamental of all safety measures: God. *How do we stay safe in an unsafe world?* What is the Christian alternative to safety-ism?

---

1 Greg Lukianoff and Jonathan Haidt, *The Coddling of the American Mind: How Good Intentions and Bad Ideas Are Setting Up a Generation for Failure* (New York: Penguin, 2018).

God Judges the Wicked to Protect His People 9:3-12

God judges wicked individuals: "When my enemies turn back, they stumble and perish before your presence. For you have maintained my just cause; you have sat on the throne, giving righteous judgment" (9:3-4).

God judges wicked nations: "You have rebuked the nations; you have made the wicked perish; you have blotted out their name forever and ever. The enemy came to an end in everlasting ruins; their cities you rooted out; the very memory of them has perished" (9:5-6).

God judges the wicked world: "The LORD sits enthroned forever; he has established his throne for justice, and he judges the world with righteousness; he judges the peoples with uprightness" (9:7-8).

God judges wicked individuals, wicked nations, and the wicked world, and he does so to protect his people. "The LORD is a stronghold for the oppressed, a stronghold in times of trouble. And those who know your name put their trust in you, for you, O LORD, have not forsaken those who seek you. Sing praises to the LORD, who sits enthroned in Zion! Tell among the peoples his deeds! For he who avenges blood is mindful of them; he does not forget the cry of the afflicted" (9:9-12).

God judges the wicked out of love for his people.

"Is there any hope for the wicked?"
Yes, because God often saves through judgment.

God Judges the Wicked to Save the Wicked 9:19-20

David concludes Psalm 9 with some hints of hope for the wicked: "Arise, O LORD! Let not man prevail; let the nations be judged before you! Put them in fear, O LORD! Let the nations know that they are but men!" (9:19-20).

He prays that God's judgments on the wicked will lead them to fear and humility before God. He asks that God put them in awe and make them realize they are mere men, weak and frail, whose anger is no match for God's. David asks that God bring them down that they might look up.

This helps us better understand Christ's seven calls for judgment on the wicked in Matthew 23. Christ does not take pleasure in the suffering of evil people. He protects his people for their good and humbles the wicked for their good. This doesn't mean all the wicked respond in the right way, but some do.

God judges the wicked out of love for the wicked.

Changing Our Story with God's Story

Praise Jesus for sacrificing his safety to save the wicked. He submitted to the greatest judgment of God to save us from judgment. He was judged as wicked so that we could be saved as righteous. He took the greatest danger to give the greatest salvation.

Summary: How do we stay safe in an unsafe world? *Praise God for giving ultimate safety, and for the judgment that saves.*

Question: How does your salvation affect your safety decisions?

Prayer: My Savior and My Safety, I take refuge in you because your judgments save me, and they even save the judged.

Comfort lessens our prayers but danger multiples them.

Hear
God's Story

Change
Your Story

Tell
the Story

Change
Others' Stories

10

Why Is God
So Quiet?

PSALM 10

Why is God so quiet when the wicked are so noisy? Why does it appear that God is nowhere to be seen, when the wicked can be seen everywhere? Why does it look as though God is slow when the wicked are busy? *Why does God delay when the wicked are so early?*

We're not the first believers to ask these questions. Three thousand years ago, the writer of Psalm 10 asked the same painful questions. Thankfully, God gave the psalmist three comforting answers.

God Delays to Multiply the Danger 10:1–11

The psalmist was desperate. From his perspective, the Lord was nowhere to be found: "Why, O Lord, do you stand far away? Why do you hide yourself in times of trouble?" (10:1).

Worse, the wicked were everywhere (10:2–11). They persecuted God's poor (10:2), boasted about breaking God's law (10:3), denied God's existence (10:4), and mocked God's judgments (10:5).

The psalmist was especially pained by what they said: "There is no God" (10:4); "I shall not be moved; throughout all generations I shall not meet adversity" (10:6); "God has forgotten, he has hidden his face, he will never see it" (10:11).

God brings us into danger to make us feel our danger. In truth, we are always in spiritual peril, but we rarely feel it as we ought. God puts us in situations where we feel our danger: the danger of our lostness, the danger of others' lostness, the danger of death, the danger of false doctrine and practice, the danger of injustice, the danger of the devil, and so on.

Believe your danger and feel your danger.

"We see the danger and God sees the danger, so why does God still delay?"
To make us pray.

God Delays to Intensify Our Prayers 10:12–15

Did the psalmist give up on God? No, after listing all the works of the wicked, he asked God to work. He asked the Lord to arise (10:12a); remember (10:12b); hear (10:13); see (10:14); break (10:15a); and pursue (10:15b). God delays to increase, intensify, deepen, and amplify our prayers. Trouble transforms our rote prayers into heartfelt prayers. Our prayers change from cold and formal to hot and emotional. They are no longer passive and fatalistic "What will be, will be" prayers. They reflect desperate yearning and intense pining.

Comfort lessens our prayers but danger multiples them.

"We've prayed, so why is God still delaying?"
To show us his power.

God Delays to Magnify His Power 10:16–18

David leaves us in no doubt as to the eventual outcome: "The LORD is king forever and ever; the nations perish from his land. O LORD, you hear the desire of the afflicted; you will strengthen their heart; you will incline your ear to do justice to the fatherless and the oppressed, so that man who is of the earth may strike terror no more" (10:16–18). The Lord reigns (10:16), the Lord hears (10:17), and the Lord delivers (10:18). God delays to magnify his power in delivering.

God minimizes us to maximize his power.

Changing Our Story with God's Story

One of the ways I worship Christ with the psalms is to imagine him singing them. Like every Jewish boy, Jesus would have learned the psalms and sung them in his home and in the synagogue. I see him in great peril, singing verses 1–11; I see him falling to his knees, praying verses 12–15; I see him rising from his knees, confidently singing about God's deliverance. No one was in greater danger, no one had greater prayers, and no one had a greater deliverance than Jesus.

When the wicked are everywhere and God seems to be nowhere, describe your great peril, pray a great prayer, and be confident of great protection.

Summary: Why does God delay when the wicked are so early? *Wait patiently, and you'll wait productively.*

Question: When has God delayed in your life, and what did you learn?

Prayer: Patient God, when I am impatient for you to work, make me sense my weakness, mature my prayers, and magnify your power.

Let scary threats take you to God's stable throne.

11

Earthquake Faith

PSALM 11

A moral and spiritual earthquake threatens the foundations of our society. Good is called evil and evil is called good. Lies are considered truth. The most basic distinctions in society are cracked and crumbling as people question: What is marriage? What is a man? What is a woman? What is a family? What is right? What is wrong?

The earthquake has hit the media, schools, businesses, courts, churches, and even our own homes. Nothing is steady and sure. Everything is shaking and quaking—including ourselves. *What can stabilize us in such unstable times?* We find a strong, steady stabilizer in Psalm 11.

The Lord Is Trustworthy 11:1-3

David's enemies were taunting him: "Flee like a bird to your mountain" (11:1). The wicked held power, and the righteous were powerless in the face of their aggression and violence. The godly were being chased out of their homes, churches, and businesses.

The wicked were telling David to flee for safety in a nearby mountain, but David knew their real intent: "Behold, the wicked bend the bow; they have fitted their arrow to the string to shoot in the dark at the upright in heart" (11:2). If the righteous ran to the mountains, they would run into an ambush.

David and his fellow believers were in dire straits. No wonder he asks, "If the foundations are destroyed, what can the righteous do?" (11:3). It looked hopeless. There weren't just hairline cracks in the fabric of society. The whole foundation was crumbling. The wicked were in power and the godly were not only being mocked but murdered. The basic essentials of a civil society had been smashed. What could the righteous do?

"In the LORD I take refuge" (11:1). David decides to run not from the wicked, but to God.

Running to the Lord is safer than simply running from the wicked.

"Why does David seek safety in God?"
Because David sees God's throne.

The Lord Is on His Throne 11:4–7

"The LORD is in his holy temple; the LORD's throne is in heaven; his eyes see, his eyelids test the children of man" (11:4). God reigns over everything, sees everything, and uses these events to test people. He tests believers to reveal their faith and faithfulness in the face of the wicked's threats. But he also tests unbelievers to reveal where their hearts really lie.

And just in case anyone thinks that the wicked's success means that God loves the wicked and hates the righteous, the psalmist confidently asserts: "[God's] soul hates the wicked and the one who loves violence" (11:5) but "loves righteous deeds" (11:7).

David predicted that God will "rain coals on the wicked; fire and sulfur and a scorching wind shall be the portion of their cup" (11:6), but "the upright shall behold God's face" (11:7). What a contrast in ends: God's face or God's fire. What a change of view for the righteous: from the wicked's face to God's face.

The scary threats of the wicked drove David to the stable throne of God. David's faith was stronger than his fears. Moral threats in society need not be spiritual earthquakes in our soul.

Let scary threats take you to God's stable throne.

Changing Our Story with God's Story

When we sing the psalms, we can sing them *to* Christ, we can sing them *of* Christ, and we can sing them *with* Christ. We can sing Psalm 11 with Christ because he died in the midst of an earthquake, both external and internal (Matt. 27:51–52). Christ sang this psalm as he took refuge from the wicked in God.

Summary: What can stabilize us when everything is shaking? *Find safety and stability in God's secure and stable throne.*

Question: What aspect of God's character stabilizes you?

Prayer: My Refuge and My King, stabilize me until I see your face.

God's pure word
protects from
the wicked's
painful words.

12

A Sound for Sore Ears

PSALM 12

"Sticks and stones may break my bones, but words will never hurt me." Really? Whoever says that has never been bullied.

A few years ago, a study conducted by research psychologists at Purdue University found that memories of painful emotional experiences linger far longer than those involving physical pain. The researchers quizzed people about painful events in the previous five years and found that it was much easier for people to relive, reexperience, and resuffer from social pain than from physical pain.[1]

What do we do when words have wounded us? We turn to the healing word of God, as the psalmist did in Psalm 12.

We Suffer from the Words of the Wicked 12:1–4

"Save, O LORD, for the godly one is gone; for the faithful have vanished from among the children of man" (12:1). Wherever David looked, the wicked were increasing while the godly were decreasing. Wicked words were multiplying while godly words were shrinking.

What's so bad about that? In contrast with the truthful, sincere, and genuine words of the godly, the wicked's words were characterized by lies, flattery, and a double heart: "Everyone utters lies to his neighbor; with flattering lips and a double heart they speak" (12:2–3). It was impossible to know when anyone was speaking the truth.

---

1 "Hurt Feelings Worse Than Pain," *BBC News*, August 29, 2008, http://news.bbc .co.uk/.

But it didn't stop there. Their tongues made great boasts: "With our tongue we will prevail, our lips are with us; who is master over us?" (12:4). They had confidence in the supremacy and success of their wicked words. It was agony for David to hear their triumphant talk.

Sticks and stones can break my bones,
but words break my heart.

"What words can heal our broken hearts?"
God's powerfully soothing words.

We Trust in the Words of God 12:5-8

The wicked have spoken, but now God speaks: "'Because the poor are plundered, because the needy groan, I will now arise,' says the LORD; 'I will place him in the safety for which he longs'" (12:5). God does not sit idly by, unconcerned as the weak and defenseless are verbally assailed and assaulted. He sees their wounds, he hears their groans, and promises protection and safety.

How does he do this? He can remove the wounded sufferer from the verbally violent circumstances. Or, as here, he can give his own healing word to replace the wounding words. "The words of the LORD are pure words, like silver refined in a furnace on the ground, purified seven times" (12:6). How the psalmist welcomed God's pure, powerful, precious, protective words.

He responded by repeating God's protective promises in the midst of the wicked's wounding words: "You, O LORD, will keep them; you will guard us from this generation forever. On every side the wicked prowl, as vileness is exalted among the children of man" (12:7-8). The psalmist walks along the road and sees vile deeds and hears vile words, but God keeps and shields him with his pure, powerful, protective word.

God's pure word protects from the wicked's painful words.

Changing Our Story with God's Story

Psalms like this must have been frequently on the lips of Jesus when he lived in this wicked world and was daily wounded with the wicked's words. And of course, he himself is the perfect word of God—pure, like silver refined in a furnace on the ground, purified seven times. We love him and we love his word, especially when we are attacked with hateful words. When someone's words remind us of their hate, we use Jesus's words to remind us of his love.

Summary: What do we do when words wound us? *We fill our ears with God's healing word to heal from the wicked's wounding words.*

Question: How will this psalm change the way you process word-wounds from the past and in the future?

Prayer: Healer of Wounds, bring your word into my life to heal me and make me a healer not a wounder.

If we question God's timing, it's time to start trusting.

Hear
God's Story

Change
Your Story

Tell
the Story

Change
Others' Stories

13

Short Answers for Long Questions

PSALM 13

"How long will this go on? How long do I have to wait? How long will this last? How long? How long? How long?"

How long? is a question we all ask, isn't it? How long will my child rebel? How long will the bullying last? How long will evil go unpunished? How long will this pain continue? How long must the chemo continue? How long will my depression last? How long must I wait for a wife/husband/friend? How long will this temptation persist? How long will this test be? How long until he forgives me? How long must I wait for assurance? How long until God takes me to heaven?

What's God's answer to our "how long" questions? In Psalm 13, God gives us three short answers to our "how long" questions.

Our Questions Are Long 13:1-4

"How long, O Lord?" is a question David often asked because he suffered many times in many ways. Look at how many ways he suffers in this psalm alone:

- *Spiritual* suffering: "How long, O Lord? Will you forget me forever? How long will you hide your face from me?" (13:1).
- *Mental* suffering: "How long must I take counsel in my soul?" (13:2a).
- *Emotional* suffering: "How long must I . . . have sorrow in my heart all the day? (13:2).

- *External* suffering: "How long shall my enemy be exalted over me?" (13:2c).
- *Potentially fatal* suffering: "Consider and answer me, O Lord my God; light up my eyes, lest I sleep the sleep of death" (13:3).
- *Social* suffering: "Lest my enemy say, 'I have prevailed over him,' lest my foes rejoice because I am shaken" (13:4). It was hard for David to face people, because of what they had been saying about him.

David was worried that his frail faith wouldn't endure the lengthy suffering he was experiencing.

Long-suffering generates long questioning.

"So what's God's answer?"
God's answers are surprisingly short and simple.

God's Answers Are Short 13:5–6

God provides David with three one-word answers, which David articulates and expresses.

The first answer is *trust*: "I have trusted in your steadfast love" (13:5a). David is reminded of how he has trusted in God's steady love in the past.

The second answer is *rejoice*: "My heart shall rejoice in your salvation" (13:5b). Whatever else he has lost, David still has God's salvation, and that alone is reason to rejoice.

The third answer is *worship*. "I will sing to the Lord, because he has dealt bountifully with me" (13:6). David can find many reasons from the past to praise God in the present.

When we ask, "How long?" God gives three short answers: Trust, rejoice, and worship. When you have long complex questions, hear God's short simple answers. Trust me. Rejoice in me. Worship me.

If we question God's timing, it's time to start trusting.

Changing Our Story with God's Story

We sing Psalm 13 to the God who experienced long-suffering himself in Jesus. Jesus suffered spiritually, mentally, emotionally, externally, and fatally. His enemies rejoiced at his sufferings and defeat. "How long?" was the cry of his soul. God's answer was short: "Long enough to save." In his human nature, Jesus trusted, rejoiced, and worshiped. Eventually God said, "That's long enough." And it was finished.

Summary: What's God's answer to our "how long" questions? *Trust, rejoice, and worship to persevere through long-suffering.*

Question: How will you answer God's answers to your "how long" questions?

Prayer: Patient God, I confess my impatience and request that you enable me to trust you, rejoice in you, and worship you, so that I can grow in patience and praise.

No sin is beyond us, because every sin is in us.

14

"I'm a Great Sinner with a Greater Savior"

PSALM 14

Toward the end of his life, the ex-slave-trader-turned-pastor John Newton said, "Although my memory's fading, I remember two things very clearly: I am a great sinner and Christ is a great Savior."[1]

If I were allowed to choose two truths that would never fade from my memory, even if aging and dementia took everything else away, I would choose: "I am a great sinner and Christ is a great Savior."

But even apart from dementia, it's easy to let these two great truths fade into forgetfulness. That's why it's important to remind ourselves of these two facts every day of our lives. So let's ask Psalm 14: "*How big a sinner am I?*" and "*How big a Savior is Christ?*"

I Am a Great Sinner 14:1–5

The first five verses of Psalm 14 read like the biographies of many of us, don't they? See if you can recognize yourself in these words:

- We were *foolish*: "The fool says in his heart, 'There is no God'" (14:1a).
- We were *foul*: "They are corrupt, they do abominable deeds; there is none who does good" (14:1b).

---

1 John Newton, *Wise Counsel: John Newton's Letters to John Ryland Jr.*, ed. Grant Gordon (Carlisle, PA: Banner of Truth, 2009), 401.

- We were *far away*: "The LORD looks down from heaven on the children of man, to see if there are any who understand, who seek after God. They have all turned aside" (14:2–3a).
- We were *filthy*: "Together they have become corrupt; there is none who does good, not even one" (14:3b).
- We were *forgetful*: "Have they no knowledge, all the evildoers . . . ?" (14:4a).
- We were *fierce*: ". . . all the evildoers who eat up my people as they eat bread and do not call upon the LORD?" (14:4b).
- We were *fearful*: "There they are in great terror, for God is with the generation of the righteous" (14:5).

Some might read these verses and say, "Well, I was never like that." That may be true. But, apart from God's preserving grace, we would have been just like that. So we can still pray these words as a true confession of what we would have been like if God had not graciously protected us from ourselves and saved us.

No sin is beyond us, because every sin is in us.

"Is there a great Savior for such a great sinner?"
Yes, there is a Savior greater than the greatest sinner.

Christ Is a Greater Savior 14:6–7

Despite verses 1–5 being true of all of us, yet, Christ is still willing and able to save those who put their trust in him and are made righteous in him. "God is with the generation of the righteous" (14:5); "The LORD is his refuge" (14:6). "Oh, that salvation for Israel would come out of Zion! When the LORD restores the fortunes of his people, let Jacob rejoice, let Israel be glad" (14:7).

Christ saves us from our folly, our foulness, our far-awayness, our filth, our forgetfulness, our ferocity, and our fears. How? By faith. He gives us faith to trust his great saving work on the cross. Great sinners can be saved by the greatest Savior.

No sinner is beyond Christ,
because no sin is bigger than Christ.

Changing Our Story with God's Story

Yes, I am a great sinner, but Christ is a great Savior, a greater Savior, the greatest Savior. Knowing how true verses 1–5 are, he still came to this earth to accomplish verses 6–7. Knowing what we were, he came to live among us, die for us, and save us. What a great Savior for great sinners. However great your sin, know that Christ is greater.

Summary: "How big a sinner am I?" "How big a Savior is Christ?" *Remember that you are a great sinner but Christ is a far greater Savior.*

Question: What truths of Jesus do you want to keep alive throughout your life?

Prayer: Great Savior, I rejoice and am glad in you because you are the greatest Savior of the greatest sinners.

A healthy devotional life is inseparable from a holy daily life.

Hear
God's Story

Change
Your Story

Tell
the Story

Change
Others' Stories

15

Daily Life and Devotional Life

PSALM 15

As Christians, we want a healthy and vigorous devotional life. We want to enjoy worshiping God in our homes and in our churches. We want to honor and please God in our worship as well as experience spiritual benefit from it ourselves. But sometimes we're not sure if this is happening. Indeed, sometimes we have no sense of pleasing God or of spiritual profit. What's going on there? What's going wrong there?

Psalm 15 answers that question and points to the solution. It's this: Our daily life is connected to our devotional life. Or, to put it another way: a healthy devotional life is inseparable from a holy daily life. *How is our daily life connected to our devotional life?*

Live a Holy Daily Life 15:1–5

David begins Psalm 15 with one of the most important questions we could ever ask: "Lord, who shall sojourn in your tent? Who shall dwell on your holy hill?" (15:1). Who can worship God? Who can live in God's holy presence? Who can worship God successfully?

The answer is not about getting the right religious practices in place. It's not about following liturgical rules. In fact, David leaves the sanctuary altogether and finds his answer not in the place of worship, but in the place of work—daily work, everyday life. Look at his description of an ideal worshiper:

- He has a blameless walk: "He who walks blamelessly" (15:2a).
- He does righteous actions: "He . . . does what is right" (15:2b).

- He speaks truthful words: "He . . . speaks truth in his heart" (15:2c).
- He loves his neighbor: "He . . . does not slander with his tongue and does no evil to his neighbor, nor takes up a reproach against his friend" (15:3).
- He's a faithful friend: "In [his] eyes a vile person is despised, but who honors those who fear the LORD" (15:4a).
- He keeps his promises: "He . . . swears to his own hurt and does not change" (15:4b).
- He's a generous giver: "He . . . does not put out his money at interest" (15:5a).
- He cannot be corrupted: "He . . . does not take a bribe against the innocent" (15:5b).

Sunday worship cannot be separated from Monday through Saturday work.

We can't hate others in our work
and then love God in our worship.

"So, what's the result of living a holy daily life?"
A healthy devotional life.

Love a Healthy Devotional Life 15:1, 5

In answer to the questions in verse 1, the holy person described in verses 2–5 will sojourn in God's tent; this godly person will dwell on God's holy hill. And, as the psalm concludes, "He who does these things shall never be moved" (15:5). A stable, steady godly life will result in a stable, steady relationship with God.

If we live a holy daily life, we will enjoy a healthy devotional life. Then, when we begin to worship, we can be confident that God accepts us, welcomes us, and says, "You can stay here." We will also enjoy a sense of spiritual strength and security. We shall never be moved.

A healthy devotional life is inseparable from a holy daily life.

Changing Our Story with God's Story

You might wonder, "But I thought we believed in salvation by grace? I thought our personal holiness had no place in our salvation?" That's true. Salvation is by grace alone by faith alone in Christ alone. Works have no place in our salvation. In fact, Christ's work in fulfilling this psalm perfectly is our salvation.

However, works do have a place in the saved life. Once saved, God connects our salvation and enjoyment of him with a holy life. If we want to love God well, we must live for God well.

Summary: How is our daily life connected to our devotional life? *Live a holy daily life for a healthy devotional life.*

Question: How have you noticed the connection between your working life and your worshiping life?

Prayer: Holy God, you want holy worshipers. Therefore give me perfect holiness in Christ and develop growing holiness in my life.

We can face death with confidence if we face death with Christ.

16

A Confidence Booster

PSALM 16

"How can I boost my confidence?" Judging by Google search results, lots of people ask that question. It's understandable, because confidence is a fantastic feeling and a huge help in life.

A deeper analysis of the Google search results reveal that most people are looking for "self-confidence" and "self-assurance." Various techniques are suggested: "Visualize yourself as you want to be"; "Affirm yourself"; "Do one thing that scares you every day"; and so on. That's all fairly nebulous, isn't it? *Are there better ways to find better confidence?*

Yes, Psalm 16 assures us that God wants us to have confidence—not self-confidence, but God-confidence that helps us both to live and to die.

God Gives Us Confidence to Live 16:1–8

"Preserve me, O God, for in you I take refuge" (16:1). Right up front, David clarifies that his confidence is not in himself but in God. He doesn't try his best, then, when that fails, try God. No, he starts with trusting in God and goes on trusting in God. "I say to the LORD, 'You are my Lord; I have no good apart from you'" (16:2). He cultivates that God-confidence through fellowship with God's people (16:3) and by fleeing false gods (16:4).

Let's listen to his confidence in God and allow it to wash over us and soak into us: "The LORD is my chosen portion and my cup; you hold my lot. The lines have fallen for me in pleasant places;

indeed, I have a beautiful inheritance. I bless the LORD who gives me counsel; in the night also my heart instructs me. I have set the LORD always before me; because he is at my right hand, I shall not be shaken" (16:5–8). Now that's unshakable confidence! Everything is sure, steady, and stable when David's confidence is in God and not himself.

Confidence comes from looking to God not self.

"Confidence in life is great, but what about the end of life?"
God also gives us confidence to die.

God Gives Us Confidence to Die 16:9–11

Although God preserved David from death many times in his life, David knew he must eventually die. But he even looked ahead to that with confidence: "My heart is glad, and my whole being rejoices!" he sings at the prospect of death (16:9).

Why? Two reasons: He knew he would be raised from the dead, and he would be happy in heaven. Listen to these confident·words: "My flesh also dwells secure. For you will not abandon my soul to Sheol [the place of the dead], or let your holy one see corruption" (16:9–10). That's resurrection. "You make known to me the path of life; in your presence there is fullness of joy; at your right hand are pleasures forevermore" (16:11). That's glorification. David is confident that his body and soul will get both eternal life and eternal joy. With the benefit of the New Testament, we know that this is possible only through Christ, who is the resurrection and the life (John 11:25).

We can face death with confidence
if we face death with Christ.

Changing Our Story with God's Story

Psalm 16 was fulfilled imperfectly in David. Like the rest of us, he didn't always have confidence in life and in death. But the apostles Peter and Paul both tell us that this psalm was fulfilled perfectly in the life, death, and resurrection of Christ (Acts 2:25–31; 13:35–37) and that David knew it would be fulfilled like that when he sang it. Go through the psalm again, hearing Christ singing it about his perfect confidence in life and death. Because Christ sang this song with confidence, we can sing this song with confidence. Because of Christ, this psalm will be fulfilled in every believer's life.

Summary: Are there better ways to find better confidence? *Boost your confidence by reducing your self-confidence and increasing your God-confidence.*

Question: How will more confidence in God benefit your life?

Prayer: You, Lord, are my confidence in life and in death. Therefore reduce my self-confidence and increase my God-confidence.

Choosing present satisfaction is choosing limited satisfaction.

17

Total Satisfaction Guaranteed

PSALM 17

"Total satisfaction guaranteed." How many times have you bought something because of that promise and ended up dissatisfied and disappointed?

Maybe Christianity has left you similarly disappointed. You became a Christian because of the promise or expectation of total satisfaction guaranteed, but it hasn't worked out that way. You're suffering, and you are far from satisfied.

Worse, non-Christians are successful and satisfied. How do we persevere? *How do we keep going in the face of disappointed expectations?* David struggled with this in Psalm 17 but eventually found a satisfying answer. Let's follow his journey from frustration to fulfillment through faith.

The Wicked's Satisfaction Is Limited 17:1–14

As David suffered at the hands of the wicked, he prayed for divine justice (17:1–4), for grace in the trial (17:5–6), and for deliverance from the wicked (17:7–14). What made the wicked's oppression so painful was that they seemed to be so happy and satisfied in their lives.

God "fill[s] their womb with treasure" (17:14), meaning their bellies are full (though not their souls). "They are satisfied with children" (17:14). Their families are full and flourishing, and they have so much stuff "they leave their abundance to their infants" (17:14).

But David reminds himself that they are "men of the world" (17:14), not men of the world to come. Their "portion is in this life" (17:14), and they will leave it all when this life ends. They have to eventually leave this world, and when they do, they will leave everything behind. Their limited satisfaction will be over and their total dissatisfaction will have begun.

Choosing present satisfaction is
choosing limited satisfaction.

"Is there an alternative to this limited and temporary satisfaction?"
Yes, the believer's satisfaction will be total and for all eternity.

The Believer's Satisfaction Will Be Total 17:15

"As for me . . . I shall be satisfied" (17:15). Having seen that the wicked's satisfaction is limited, David realizes that the believer's satisfaction *will be* total and complete. How did he get there? He overcame suffering by sampling the total satisfaction guaranteed at the end.

We will be satisfied because we will awake (17:15). To the bereaved, the believer's death looks like falling into a deep sleep. But for believers, death transports them into a whole new level of consciousness.

We will be satisfied because we will see Christ. "As for me, I shall behold your face in righteousness" (17:15). What a face we will see when we open our eyes in heaven. We will see the happiest, most beautiful, friendliest, and loveliest face ever. We will see Christ's smiling, welcoming face. What satisfaction!

We will be satisfied because we will be like Christ. "When I awake, I shall be satisfied with your likeness" (17:15). Or as the apostle John put it, "When he appears we shall be like him, because we shall see him as he is" (1 John 3:2). The moment we see Christ, we will be like him. Instead of sin, perfect holiness. Instead of suffering, perfect comfort. Instead of sadness, joy. Instead of ugliness, beauty. Instead of dissatisfaction, total satisfaction guaranteed. We will be satisfied.

Choosing eternal satisfaction is
choosing unlimited satisfaction.

Changing Our Story with God's Story

What a death! What a hope! What a satisfaction! We are totally satisfied and Christ is totally satisfied. Let's use this psalm to sample that satisfaction by faith today and motivate us to keep going. When dissatisfaction threatens us, let's sample the final satisfaction and repeat, "I will be satisfied. I will be satisfied."

Summary: How do we keep going in the face of disappointed expectations? *Overcome present suffering by sampling the total satisfaction guaranteed at the end.*

Question: Where are you tempted to seek satisfaction, and how can you get more satisfaction in Christ?

Prayer: Satisfying God, continue to be my complete satisfaction so that you will also be my forever satisfaction.

Christ was paid for his work so we could be paid without work.

Hear
God's Story

Change
Your Story

Tell
the Story

Change
Others' Stories

18

The Final Score

PSALM 18

"Don't tell me the score!"

I wanted to watch the soccer game I had recorded without knowing the final result. Unfortunately, my younger sister did what younger sisters do. She blurted out the final score. Although initially I was angry, I must admit I actually enjoyed the game more because I wasn't so anxious about the result. I didn't yell at the TV, and my blood pressure stayed low. Knowing the final score of the game transformed the whole experience for the better.

How does knowing the final score of life change our whole experience of life? We can preview the final score of life in Psalm 18.

God Reveals the Messiah

God designed the character, life, and work of Old Testament leaders as predictive pictures of the coming Messiah, so Israel would be able to recognize him when he came.

We see this in King David's life in three ways. First, sometimes David's life and character *paralleled* the Messiah's. Second, sometimes David's life was a *platform* for the Messiah. He started writing about himself, but then, inspired by the Spirit, had "liftoff" to another realm, to someone who cannot be paralleled. Third, sometimes David made direct *predictions* about the Messiah, describing events with no parallel in his life (e.g., Pss. 2; 110).

Psalm 18 falls into the second category. It's a platform psalm. David started writing about his victory over his enemies, but then from that platform soared far higher to the ultimate deliverer's character and victory.

Read David's story to recognize the deliverer's story.

"Where do we see the deliverer's story in David's story?"
In his rescue from death.

God Rescues the Messiah 18:1–19

"I love you, O Lord, my strength" (18:1). Why did David love the Lord? Because God was his fortress, deliverer, rock, refuge, shield, horn, and stronghold (18:2). Therefore, when he called upon the Lord, God saved him from his enemies (18:3).

It's at this point that David "lifts off." His great love, trust, prayer, and deliverance (18:1–3) was the platform for considering the Messiah's greatest love, trust, prayer, and deliverance (18:4–19). The divine rescue in verses 7–19 far exceeds anything God ever did in David's life. David looked down the road of time and saw the earthquakes, smoke, fire, darkness, thunder, and lightning of Calvary. But he also saw Christ's glorious resurrection: "He brought me out into a broad place; he rescued me, because he delighted in me" (18:19).

God rescued the Messiah by resurrecting the Messiah.

"Why did God rescue the Messiah?"
To reward him for his work.

God Rewards the Messiah 18:20–50

The Messiah's reward was earned, merited, and deserved. Because of his righteousness, his purity, faithfulness, obedience, and innocence (18:20–26), God rewarded him with victory at Calvary (18:27–29). But verses 31–50 look ahead to a victory greater than anything yet seen. It's looking toward the ultimate victory God will give the Messiah over all his enemies at the end of time. No wonder the last verses say: "I will praise you, O Lord, among the nations, and sing to your name. Great salvation he brings to his king, and shows steadfast love to his anointed, to David and his offspring forever" (18:49–50).

Christ was paid for his work so
we could be paid without work.

Changing Our Story with God's Story

Don't you love God's providence and how he designed the Old Testament to prepare for, predict, and picture the future Messiah? Psalms like this one put Christ on the platform and applause in our hearts.

Summary: How does knowing the final score of life change our whole experience of life? *Remember the final score to keep calm and relaxed even when Christ's enemies appear to be winning.*

Question: How can you better remember the final score, and how will that change your present life?

Prayer: Victorious God, thank you for not only winning a great victory in Christ but for inviting me to share in that victory now through faith in Christ.

God's world
and God's word
transform our world
and our words.

19

God's Solution for God's Silence

PSALM 19

When suffering pain or loss, we may feel as though God has abandoned us. Questions like, "Why is God absent?" and "Why is God silent?" add to our agony. "If ever I needed God's voice and God's presence, it's now. Instead . . . there's nothing."

Most Christians go through this experience of feeling abandoned and deserted at some point in their lives, causing them deep distress and even despair.

David understood this, and, in Psalm 19, opens two books God wrote to fill our void with his voice, and our holes with his holiness. *Which two books bring God's voice to us in a transforming way?*

God's World Tells of God's Glory 19:1–6

The heavens are an open book with the same three words on every page: God is glorious (19:1). Every sunrise and sunset turns a new page, each printed with the same three words: God is glorious (19:2). As the biggest book ever written, its pages are visible and readable to all people all the time (19:3–6). God's galaxies tell of God's glory. The more galaxies we discover, the more we see God's creation glory.

God is everywhere, even when we feel he is nowhere.

"I'm happy to see God's glory in God's world.
But I also need God's grace. Where can I see this?"
Open God's second book.

God's Word Tells of God's Grace 19:7-14

David turns from God's world to God's word. Although his eyes fall from massive planets to thin pages, his soul soars higher in praise.

He praises God by giving his word six titles: the law of the Lord, the testimony of the Lord, the precepts of the Lord, the commandment of the Lord, the fear of the Lord (because that is what his word produces), and the rules of the Lord (19:7-9).

He praises God for six qualities of his word. It is perfect, sure, right, pure, clean, and true (7-9).

He praises God for six accomplishments of his word. It saves souls, makes the simple profound, makes the sad happy, gives clarity to the confused, cleans the dirty forever, and creates godly character and conduct (19:7-9).

Finally, David gets more personal, testifying to six ways he experienced God's word. It was precious to him; it was a pleasure to him; it protected him; it profited him; it produced fruit in him; and it promoted praise from him (19:10-14). Six titles, six qualities, six accomplishments, and six experiences of God's word. But one message is in and through it all: God is gracious.

God's word of grace lead to words to praise: "Let the words of my mouth and the meditation of my heart be acceptable in your sight, O Lord, my rock and my redeemer" (19:14).

God's world and God's word transform our world and our words.

Changing Our Story with God's Story

Praise God that his physical world declares his glory and his written word declares his grace. Then go further and remember that Christ is the Creator of the world and he is the incarnate word. We see Christ's glory in his creation and his grace in the incarnation. The glory of God's truth and grace is seen most brightly in the Word made flesh.

If we shut our eyes to Christ's world and our ears to Christ's word, we will find God to be absent and silent. But if we open our eyes to his world and our ears to his word, we will have God and hear God no matter what we're going through. In Psalm 19, God assures us that he is never silent or absent.

Summary: Which two books bring God's voice to us in a transforming way? *Open the books of Christ's world and Christ's word to bring God near in a world-and-word-transforming way.*

Question: Which of God's two books do you need to open more, and why?

Prayer: Glorious and Gracious God, thank you for your world and for your word's transformational power.

Our salvation hangs on an unbreakable thread.

20

Total Trust for Real Rest

PSALM 20

I find it hard to relinquish control of a car to someone else. It's not that I don't trust other drivers. I do . . . but not totally. I trust them enough to let them drive, but not enough to let them drive without my input, and certainly not enough for me to fall asleep while they're driving.

It's hard to give up all control and totally trust someone else when our lives are on the line. That's especially true when it comes to our salvation. It's difficult to completely trust Jesus Christ to safely "drive" us all the way to heaven without our input or help. It's often a battle to relax and rest entirely upon him. But when we do, our journey is much more peaceful and enjoyable.

How can we give total trust and get total rest? Psalm 20 prizes our hands off the steering wheel and our foot off the pedals by guiding us to enjoy real rest in our souls by total trust in Christ.

Our Salvation Is Suspended on Our King 20:1–6

The title of Great Britain's national anthem is "God Save the King." This is also a phrase that concludes royal proclamations, and is a common toast at ceremonial dinners. It's a prayer by which the British recognize that their health and prosperity are bound up with the king's.

Psalm 20 was one of Israel's national anthems, a song in which the nation prayed for the king's health and prosperity in order to secure their own. But this song wasn't about just an earthly king; it was also about God's special King, his anointed, the Messiah (20:6).

It was more than a national anthem; it was a spiritual anthem that believers sang to express how their salvation was entirely bound up in the coming Christ.

That's why the singers prayed for God to protect the king from trouble (20:1), support the king in trouble (20:2), accept the king's sacrifices (20:3), hear the king's prayers, and accomplish the king's plans (20:4). Confident this would happen, the singers shouted about their salvation and joyfully waved victory flags of celebration (20:5).

Our salvation hangs on an unbreakable thread.

"But I need to know more about this security before I can have certainty." Keep listening to this anthem.

Our Salvation Is Secured by Our King 20:6-9

The singers were convinced that God would save and secure his anointed (20:6). Although others trusted in military strategies and military might, they trusted in the name of the Lord their God. They knew all human efforts would fail and fall, but those who trusted God would stand with the king in victory (20:7-8). The psalm therefore ends with one great prayer: "O LORD, save the king" (20:9), because they knew that the salvation of the king secured their salvation too.

99 percent trust = 1 percent rest.
100 percent trust = 100 percent rest.

Changing Our Story with God's Story

Living on the other side of Calvary, we no longer have to pray "God save the King!" Instead, we can praise, "God saved the King!" In doing so, he saved us too. God protected and supported King Jesus, accepted his sacrifice, and accomplished his plans. We therefore can joyfully shout about salvation and wave victory flags of celebration. We offer no input or assistance, we turn from all human might and wisdom, and we totally trust in the victorious name of the Lord our God. We totally trust and therefore really rest. Backseat resting is so much better than backseat driving.

Summary: How can we give total trust and get total rest? *We enjoy real rest in our soul by totally trusting in Christ.*

Question: What hinders your trust and therefore your rest? What can increase your trust and your rest?

Prayer: Saving King, save your subjects who give you their trust by giving them your rest.

Jesus enjoys saving sinners.

Hear
God's Story

Change
Your Story

Tell
the Story

Change
Others' Stories

21

Catching the King's Contagious Joy

PSALM 21

Neuroscientists at University College London have found that laughter is contagious.[1] Using MRI scanners, researchers discovered that the brain responds to the sound of laughter by telling our face muscles to join in the joy. When we see someone laughing, chances are we also will smile.

Can we use that research to "catch" spiritual joy? *Can we increase the joy of salvation by "catching" it from someone else?*

Yes, as Psalm 21 demonstrates, King David "caught" the joy of salvation by seeing and hearing King Jesus's joy in salvation. And he turns to us and says: Enjoy more joy in your salvation by enjoying the King's joy in your salvation.

King Jesus Celebrates His Defeat of Death 21:1-7

As David opens a palace window for us, we peek in, see a scene we can never unsee, and exclaim: "O Lord, in your strength the king rejoices, and in your salvation how greatly he exults!" (21:1). We see unimaginable joy and jubilation. The King could not be happier. Why? God answered his greatest prayer, crowned him with the greatest crown, and blessed him with the greatest blessings (21:2-3).

---

1   Daryl Austin, "Laughter Really Is Contagious—and That's Good," *The Washington Post*, January 15, 2023, https://www.washingtonpost.com/.

His greatest prayer was for life after death: "He asked life of you; you gave it to him, length of days forever and ever" (21:4). His greatest crown was the salvation of sinners: "His glory is great through your salvation; splendor and majesty you bestow on him" (21:5). His greatest blessing was his heavenly reward: "For you make him most blessed forever; you make him glad with the joy of your presence" (21:6). What carried him from the depths of death to the heights of heaven? Faith and love. "For the king trusts in the LORD, and through the steadfast love of the Most High he shall not be moved" (21:7).

Who is this happy King? King David certainly had his moments of celebration, but this transcends any human experience. David's limited victories and joys gave him prophetic insight into the greater victories and greater joys of his future greatest Son and the Son's greatest joy in saving sinners from sin and death.

Jesus enjoys saving sinners.

"Jesus defeated death, but his enemies are still busy and active. Will he ever defeat them?" Listen to his victory celebrations.

King Jesus Celebrates His Defeat of His Enemies 21:8–13

Having opened the palace window to show us the King celebrating his victory over death, the psalmist then opens a prophetic window to show us the King's future victory over his enemies.

No matter how far they run, his antennae will find all who hate him (21:8). No matter how big they are, his fire will swallow them (21:9). No matter how many there are, his judgment will destroy them (21:10). No matter how successful they were, their success is over (21:11–12)

The King's strength guarantees success for his followers and defeat for his enemies: "Be exalted, O LORD, in your strength! We will sing and praise your power" (21:13). The more the psalmist sees of the King's joy, the more his joy increases. This is contagious healing.

Get more present joy by seeing
Jesus's future joy.

Changing Our Story with God's Story

Open a window of joy in your own heart by opening a window into Jesus's joyful heart. See his joy in defeating death and all opposition to his people. May we catch this joy from him, that others may catch it from us.

Summary: Can we increase the joy of salvation by "catching" it from someone else? *We can enjoy more joy in our salvation by enjoying the King's joy in our salvation.*

Question: How happy do you think Jesus is to save you?

Prayer: Joyful Jesus, share your happiness in salvation with me so that I may catch it and spread it to others.

Hell on earth erupted upon heaven's Son.

22

Deepest Suffering for Highest Glory

PSALM 22

Pain can be so deep and last so long that we lose heart. We give up and give in. "I just can't go on. I can't live another day like this," we groan. *How do we regain heart? How can we get up and get going again?*

When the Corinthian Christians hit rock-bottom, the apostle Paul encouraged their hearts by raising their eyes: "So we do not lose heart. . . . For this light momentary affliction is preparing for us an eternal weight of glory beyond all comparison" (2 Cor. 4:16–17). He invigorated their empty and sagging hearts with this truth: the deeper the earthly suffering, the higher the heavenly glory.

Christ was the premier example of this, as we see in Psalm 22, a psalm that predicted Christ's suffering so accurately that Christ had it on his lips in his deepest suffering (Matt. 27:46).

Suffering Punctures Our Heart 22:1–21

Heaven and hell united against Christ to plunge a double-edged dagger into his heart.

The first serrated edge was the feeling that God had abandoned him. Christ experienced the desolation of divine desertion. We can imagine Christ thinking the following: I am groaning while God has abandoned me (22:1); I am praying but God does not answer me (22:2); I am trusting but God does not deliver me from shame (22:5–10); I need help but God is nowhere to be found (22:11). Dependent on God yet deserted by God, resting on God yet rejected by God. How horrific for God's uniquely beloved Son.

The second jagged edge was the realization that the powers of hell surrounded him. We can imagine Jesus feeling as though he were surrounded by herds of strong bulls (22:12), ravening and roaring lions (22:13), wild dogs (22:16, 20), and wild oxen (22:21). Gnashing teeth savaged him and thrusting horns mauled him. These were not literal animals but descriptions of how the most barbaric demons of hell came through the worst of men to destroy the best of men.

Hell on earth erupted upon heaven's Son.

"How did Christ restore his punctured heart?"
Psalm 22 predicts the restoration.

Glory Animates Our Heart 22:22–31

Christ healed his heart by looking past the sufferings of hell to the worship of heaven. His heart burst with praise as he anticipated leading the throngs of heaven in songs of praise.

"I will tell of your name to my brothers; in the midst of the congregation I will praise you" (22:22). "You who fear the LORD, praise him! All you offspring of Jacob, glorify him, and stand in awe of him, all you offspring of Israel!" (22:23). "From you comes my praise in the great congregation; my vows I will perform before those who fear him" (22:25). "The afflicted shall eat and be satisfied; those who seek him shall praise the LORD! May your hearts live forever!" (22:26). "All the ends of the earth shall remember and turn to the LORD, and all the families of the nations shall worship before you" (22:27). By the end of the psalm Christ has given us sixteen different descriptions of heavenly praise. No greater pain; no higher praise. No deeper hell; no higher heaven.

Christ lost everything,
but he didn't lose heart.

Changing Our Story with God's Story

This psalm gives us a glimpse into Christ's soul as he suffered on the cross. Dagger after dagger was plunged with fury into his heart, but he worked furiously to not lose heart. When we lose heart, we know that our Savior is able to sympathize with us. Let's not lose heart but keep our hearts full of praise and fellowship. And let's join Jesus by looking ahead to the joys of heavenly glory.

Summary: How do you regain heart? How can you get up and get going again? *When your heart is punctured by great grief, heal your heart by gazing on greater glory.*

Question: Do you know some believers whom you can help to encourage their soul with this devotional message?

Prayer: Glorious Lord and Savior, I lift my eyes to the highest heavens to see and hear your praises so that my soul will be lifted out of the depths.

Wherever there's a seeking sheep, there's a seeking shepherd.

23

An American Dream Comes True

PSALM 23

Ten years into marriage, Patrick and Jen had drifted from God and from one another. They'd pursued the American dream, but it had mutated into an awful nightmare. Yes, they had two successful careers, two new cars, and two beautiful children. But they had lost their love for God and for one another. They had everything, yet had nothing. They lacked nothing, yet lacked everything. God was teaching them that we will lack, lose, and get lost when we follow anyone other than the Lord. But they weren't listening or learning.

Patrick's father died of a heart attack, and the first song at his funeral was Psalm 23. Although Patrick had sung it many times before, this time he couldn't get past the first line: "The LORD is my shepherd; I shall not want" (23:1). He realized that neither statement was true in his life. The Lord was not his shepherd, and he had many wants. *How is having a shepherd and having no wants connected?* Patrick asked himself as he felt an aching hollowness within.

Over the coming weeks he studied Psalm 23 with Jen as they rededicated their lives to being shepherded by Christ. As they did so, Psalm 23 opened up to them, teaching them three valuable truths.

Our Shepherd Leads Us through Life 23:1-3

Lying down, green pastures, still waters, restored souls, and righteous paths were distant memories for Patrick and Jen (23:2-3). Endless running, arid wastes, polluted pools, drained souls, and sinful patterns made up their present painful reality. Having abandoned their shepherd's leading in life, Patrick and Jen were lost and lifeless. But they came as lost sheep and found a seeking shepherd.

Wherever there's a seeking sheep,
there's a seeking shepherd.

"What about the end of life?"
Our shepherd never leaves us.

Our Shepherd Leads Us through Death 23:4

Patrick's father was a fit fifty-five-year-old, yet death took him suddenly without warning. Patrick hadn't realized how much he leaned on his dad until he was no longer there to bear his weight. The world felt dark, lonely, and scary. Jen comforted Patrick through long, anxious, sleepless nights with these words: "Even though I walk through the valley of the shadow of death, I will fear no evil, for you are with me; your rod and your staff, they comfort me" (23:4). Psalm 23 offers us this special promise of special shepherding through death.

Our shepherd will never forsake us,
so we should never fear.

"Our shepherd is with us in life and in death,
but what's on the other side of death?"
Our shepherd is there also.

Our Shepherd Leads Us Home 23:6

Over many months, the Lord reoriented Patrick and Jen's lives. As they followed the good shepherd, goodness and mercy followed them all the days of their lives. They no longer lived for themselves and for the moment, but for the Lord and for eternity. They lived with him and for him, and had a new assurance that they would live with him and for him forever (23:6). Now that's a dream come true.

Live with Christ now, and
you'll live with Christ forever.

Changing Our Story with God's Story

Jesus said, "I am the good shepherd. The good shepherd lays down his life for the sheep.... I am the good shepherd. I know my own and my own know me, just as the Father knows me and I know the Father; and I lay down my life for the sheep" (John 10:11, 14–15). Jesus leads us in life, through death, and all the way home. Even in heaven he will continue to lead us, and we will follow him perfectly forever.

Summary: How is having a shepherd and having no wants connected? *Follow the Lord's leading, and you'll never lack, never lose, and never get lost.*

Question: In what ways is Jesus shepherding you today?

Prayer: Good Shepherd, shepherd me closely so that I never lack, never lose, and never get lost.

Our King sparkles
in his victory
and dazzles in
his humanity.

24

Empowering Praise

PSALM 24

I vividly remember the first time I visited Washington, DC. Everything seemed to have been designed and laid out with one word in mind: *power*. I imagined George Washington giving his architects a one-word plan: *power*. I imagine he instructed, "Build a city that says *power* wherever you look." The master plan was a masterstroke as the physical projection of power in the infant nation's capital both assured its friends and intimidated its enemies.

How does King Jesus assure his friends and intimidate his enemies? Open Psalm 24, and join a tour of Christ's kingdom.

Christ Is King of the World 24:1–2

Whatever title deeds and border signs say, the Bible says that Christ owns the whole world—everything and everyone in it: "The earth is the LORD's and the fullness thereof, the world and those who dwell therein" (24:1). How can Christ make such a claim? He made it; therefore, he owns it. "For he has founded it upon the seas, and established it upon the rivers" (24:2).

Christ owns every atom because he made every atom.

"He owns the world, but does he have a favorite place in the world?" *Yes, he loves his church more than anywhere else.*

Christ Is King of the Church 24:3–5

"Who shall ascend the hill of the LORD? And who shall stand in his holy place?" (24:3). The church is the Lord's holy place. As owner, our royal King sets royal standards for his royal children in his royal palace. "He who has clean hands and a pure heart, who does not lift up his soul to what is false and does not swear deceitfully" (24:4). These are high and holy standards, but they result in high and holy blessings. "He will receive blessing from the LORD and righteousness from the God of his salvation" (24:5).

The King's kids carry out the King's commands for the King's crown.

"The King's kids are truly blessed, but what reward does Christ get for all his work?" He gets even greater glory and honor.

Christ Is King of Heaven 24:8–10

Having asserted ownership of his earthly kingdom, and claimed his spiritual kingdom, the King collects his eternal kingdom. When he knocks on the door, angels ask, "Who is this King of glory?" Other angels reply, "The LORD, strong and mighty, the LORD, mighty in battle!" (24:8) In unison, they exclaim: "Lift up your heads, O gates! And lift them up, O ancient doors, that the King of glory may come in" (24:9). As he enters in triumph, angels continue to ponder and wonder: "Who is this King of glory? The LORD of hosts, he is the King of glory!" (24:10). They'd never seen him so gloriously triumphant, or so gloriously human. He remains glorious and triumphant in heaven's glories today, waiting until all his enemies have been made his footstool.

Our King sparkles in his victory and dazzles in his humanity.

Changing Our Story with God's Story

Power! Wherever we look in Christ's kingdom—the earth, the church, or heaven—we see and sense power. This power impresses and assures Christ's friends and intimidates and alarms Christ's enemies. If you are impressed and assured by this power, rejoice in your King. If you are intimidated and alarmed by this power, repent to your King.

Summary: How does Christ assure his friends and intimidate his enemies? *When you feel weak and intimidated, tour Christ's triple kingdom to be triply empowered by Christ's triple power.*

Question: How does Christ's power assure you or worry you?

Prayer: King of the World, King of the Church, and King of Heaven, thank you for assuring your friends with your power and for intimidating your enemies into fear and silence.

Disobedience results in disorientation.

25

Direction for the Disoriented

PSALM 25

As a boy, I loved our family summer vacations in the south of England. But I hated getting there. Even though we went to the same place every year, and my father carefully plotted and planned our journey beforehand, we almost always ended up lost somewhere in the middle of nowhere in the middle of the night.

Our huge fold-out paper maps didn't have a "location" button. So our problem wasn't just that we didn't know where to go; we didn't even know where we were! We didn't know where to turn, because we didn't know where we'd taken a wrong turn. If only we knew where we'd gone wrong, then we could put it right. It was all so frustrating, confusing, and disorienting.

Even if we don't know what a fold-out map is, all of us know the confusion and frustration of spiritual disorientation. So did King David. *How do we get reoriented?* Let's see how God reoriented David in Psalm 25.

Sin Disorients Us 25:4–18

Three times in this psalm, David cycles through God's guidance and our sin: God's guidance (25:4–5) and our sin (25:6–7); God's guidance (25:8–10) and our sin (25:11); God's guidance (25:12–14) and our sin (25:15–18).

David was clearly connecting disobedience and disorientation. How did we get so disoriented? We got here by sin. David repeatedly confesses his sin: "Remember not the sins of my youth or my transgressions" (25:7); "For your name's sake, O LORD, pardon my guilt, for it is great" (25:11); "Consider my affliction and my trouble, and forgive all my sins" (25:18).

Disobedience results in disorientation.

"That's how I got here, but how do I get out of here?"
We get lost. God finds us.

God Directs Us 25:4–12

David's confession of disobedience and his subsequent experience of disorientation explains his triple focus on God's guidance: "Make me to know your ways, O LORD; teach me your paths. Lead me in your truth and teach me" (25:4–5); "Good and upright is the LORD; therefore he instructs sinners in the way. He leads the humble in what is right, and teaches the humble his way. All the paths of the LORD are steadfast love and faithfulness" (25:8–10); "Who is the man who fears the LORD? Him will he instruct in the way that he should choose" (25:12).

Notice how David's words move from a prayer for God's guidance to confidence in God's guidance. He assures us that God always answers the prayer for guidance back into his holy ways with a *yes*.

God loves to guide the lost.

Changing Our Story with God's Story

Jesus said, "I am the way, and the truth, and the life" (John 14:6). He is the fulfillment of Psalm 25. If we follow his way, we will know the truth and experience life. He is God's GPS. If we come to him, he will tell us exactly where we are in relation to God, and take us safely home to life. Jesus moves us from guilt, pain, and shame to gratitude, praise, and salvation.

Summary: How do we get reoriented? *When sin disorients us, we ask Jesus to direct us to himself and his ways.*

Question: How has God redirected you when you got lost?

Prayer: My God and My Guide, I'm sorry for getting lost so often and so badly. Please redirect and reorient me so that I know where I am and where I am going.

Consistent love fuels a consistent life.

26

"The Church Is Full of Hypocrites"

PSALM 26

"The church is full of hypocrites." This is one of the most common excuses people use to avoid thinking about the claims of Christianity. They excuse their rejection of Christ with Christian hypocrisy. They don't believe because, they say, Christians are just actors, pretenders, and living contradictions.

How do we live in such a way that the accusation of hypocrisy is false, the charge doesn't stick, and we're found innocent? *How do we live for Christ in such a way that others want life from Christ?* The answer, says Psalm 26, is *integrity*, which means that our outward lives match our inner beliefs. Hypocrisy is all about living a contradiction; integrity is all about living consistently.

Integrity Is Living before God Consistently   26:1–2, 11–12

David begins this psalm by defending and protesting his life of integrity: "Vindicate me, O Lord, for I have walked in my integrity, and I have trusted in the Lord without wavering" (26:1). He is so confident that he is the genuine article, the real thing, that he invites God to look deeply into his soul and examine what is there: "Prove me, O Lord, and try me; test my heart and my mind" (26:2). His outward life has been consistent with his inward life. His lifestyle has matched his morals.

At the end of the psalm, David looks forward to his future integrity: "But as for me, I shall walk in my integrity; redeem me, and be gracious to me. My foot stands on level ground; in the great assembly

I will bless the LORD" (26:11–12). He hopes that integrity will characterize his life in the future on earth and is confident it will be his constant experience in heaven.

A Christian life is a consistent life.

"How can we be so confident in our integrity?"
That's where the middle of the psalm helps us.

Integrity Is Loving God Consistently 26:3–10

How did David maintain integrity throughout his life? First, David had a deep, private love for God: "For your steadfast love is before my eyes, and I walk in your faithfulness" (26:3). By keeping God's love before his eyes, David kept all masks off his face and life. You cannot love God without hating sin. You cannot have integrity without hating hypocrisy. That's why David goes on to say, "I do not sit with men of falsehood, nor do I consort with hypocrites. I hate the assembly of evildoers, and I will not sit with the wicked" (26:4–5, see also 26:9–10).

Second, David maintained his integrity by his public love for God: "I wash my hands in innocence and go around your altar, O LORD, proclaiming thanksgiving aloud, and telling all your wondrous deeds. O LORD, I love the habitation of your house and the place where your glory dwells" (26:6–8). This is the Old Testament vocabulary of worship. David needed public worship to maintain private worship.

Consistent love fuels a consistent life.

Changing Our Story with God's Story

Sadly, David did not live up to this psalm all his life. He lost his life of integrity because he lost his love of integrity. Only one person has ever lived up to this psalm: Jesus Christ. So, when we sing it, we're singing about him and his perfect integrity, which covers all of our hypocrisy and inconsistent consistency. But we're also using that as our power and motive to live with more integrity. Let's love the Christ who lived this psalm perfectly for us, and pray for a life of loving God consistently so that we can live before God consistently.

Summary: How do we live for Christ in such a way that others want life from Christ? *We live before God consistently by loving God consistently.*

Question: How can you increase integrity and reduce inconsistency?

Prayer: Consistent God, cover my inconsistency with Christ's consistency and give me more of Christ's consistency so that I can be a better witness for Christ.

God's beautiful face gives beautiful faith.

27

"If I Had One Prayer..."

PSALM 27

If God came to you and said, "I'll grant you one prayer request," what would you ask for? That's a revealing question isn't it? It helps us discover our highest priority, our deepest longing, and our hidden motivation. And that's good, because our priorities, longings, and motivations often influence and control us without our realizing it.

So, *what would you ask for if you had only one prayer?* In Psalm 27, King David tells us what he asked for when given this prayer opportunity.

Ugly Fears Drain Our Confidence 27:1–3

"The LORD is my light and my salvation; whom shall I fear?" (27:1). This is the essence of the entire psalm. God's light and salvation expel David's fear and consternation as he faces both external and internal enemies. Out there are foes, and in here are fears—but God reigns everywhere.

Note how many times David mentions foes and fears in the first three verses. His self-confidence has drained away in the face of ferocious opposition. But his God-confidence fills up fast as he sees God's face more than he sees his enemies: "Though war arise against me, yet I will be confident" (27:3).

Fear empties our confidence,
but faith fills us with God-confidence.

"So how did he refuel with God-confidence?"
With God's beauty.

God's Beauty Gives Us Confidence 27:4–14

"One thing have I asked of the LORD, that will I seek after: that I may dwell in the house of the LORD all the days of my life, to gaze upon the beauty of the LORD and to inquire in his temple" (27:4). Given one prayer, David asked to go to church! On the run from enemies, when given one wish, he didn't hesitate: "If I could have one thing, it would be to go to church for the rest of my life!"

But David didn't go to church just to go to church. He went to church "to gaze upon the beauty of the LORD." As God's word was read, praises were sung, prayers were offered, sermons were preached, and fellowship was enjoyed, David's one aim is "to gaze upon the beauty of the LORD" (27:4).

This theme repeats as a chorus throughout the rest of the psalm. David's ugly fears are expelled by God's beautiful face and replaced with joyful confidence. Listen to some of the beautiful words produced by God's beautiful face even in the middle of ugly times: "I will offer in his tent sacrifices with shouts of joy; I will sing and make melody to the LORD" (27:6); "You have said, 'Seek my face.' My heart says to you, 'Your face, LORD, do I seek.'" Hide not your face from me" (27:8–9); "I believe that I shall look upon the goodness of the LORD in the land of the living! Wait for the LORD; be strong, and let your heart take courage; wait for the LORD!" (27:13–14). When ugliness abounds, beauty much more abounds.

God's beautiful face gives beautiful faith.

Changing Our Story with God's Story

Where do we see the beautiful face of God most beautifully? In the face of Jesus Christ. "God . . . has shone in our hearts to give the light of the knowledge of the glory of God in the face of Jesus Christ" (2 Cor. 4:6). As Jesus said, "Whoever has seen me has seen the Father" (John 14:9). Although we cannot now see Christ's physical face with our physical eyes, the Bible has been designed in such a way that it gives us spiritual sight of our Savior with spiritual eyes.

Summary: What would you ask for if you had only one prayer? *See God's beauty in Christ's beautiful face because God's beauty expels ugly fears.*

Question: If granted one prayer request, what would you ask for?

Prayer: Beautiful God, show me your beauty and open my eyes to gaze upon you, so that my ugly fears will be expelled.

When we think God's not listening, we stop speaking.

28

Is God Listening?

"You're not listening to me." What spouse hasn't heard these words? Some of us have heard them many times. Of course, we're listening. It just *looks* like we're not. Others just don't realize how good we are at listening while we're doing something else at the same time. We can read texts while listening to others. We can watch a game while listening. We want them to believe us when we protest, "Of course I'm listening to you. It just looks like I'm not." But they're skeptical unbelievers. So they stop speaking until we start listening. Or, rather, they stop speaking until we *look* like we're listening.

Something like this can happen in our relationship with God. At times it looks as though God isn't listening to us. We pray and pray and pray, but it feels as if all our words are landing on deaf ears. We think God isn't listening, so we stop speaking. We go into "silent stare" mode. *How do we get out of "silent stare" mode and into believing prayer mode?* David shows us how in Psalm 28.

God's Seeming Silence Stops Our Prayers 28:1-5

In Psalm 28:1-2, we feel David's anguish over his fear that God's not listening to him: "To you, O Lord, I call; my rock, be not deaf to me, lest, if you be silent to me, I become like those who go down to the pit. Hear the voice of my pleas for mercy, when I cry to you for help, when I lift up my hands toward your most holy sanctuary" (28:1-2).

He's crying out, but he feels shut out. He's calling, but it appears that God's not listening. David is far from silent, but he thinks God is silent and far away. David's enemies have never been louder (28:3–5), but God has never been quieter. If this goes on much longer, the king's prayers are going to die. His prayers will be as lively as a corpse.

**When we think God's not listening,
we stop speaking.**

*"How can we get out of 'silent stare' mode?" By faith.
By believing God's ears are open, even when they appear shut.*

God's Open Ears Increase Our Prayers 28:6–9

David's prayers resurrect and rise from the grave with new life in verses 6–7: "Blessed be the LORD! For he has heard the voice of my pleas for mercy. The LORD is my strength and my shield; in him my heart trusts, and I am helped; my heart exults, and with my song I give thanks to him."

"He has heard, he is hearing, and he will hear," resurrected faith insists. God's open ears open David's mouth. He joyfully praises God with a tsunami of song. He happily paints God in multiple pictures; the Lord is David's strength, shield, song, shelter, and shepherd (28:7–9).

Faith turns silent stares into singing songs.

Changing Our Story with God's Story

Let's turn our silent stares into singing songs. God has never closed his ears to any of his praying children, because he cannot close his heart to any them. Their pleas tug at his heart, move his heart, and open his heart. Although it may look as though he's not listening, he's always listening. He listens intently. Let God's open ears increase your prayers.

Whenever I doubt whether God's ears are open to my prayers, I always think of the open wounds of Christ. If God opened Christ's wounds to save me, will he not open his ears to hear me?

Summary: How do we get out of "silent stare" mode and into believing prayer mode? *Believing God is listening will increase our speaking. Or to put it more simply: God's open ears increase our prayers.*

Question: How will this psalm change your prayers today?

Prayer: Hearer and Answerer of Prayer, help me to believe that your ears are open to listen so that my mouth is open to pray.

Our lives say either "Glory to God" or "Glory to me."

29

"Glory to Me in the Highest!"

PSALM 29

We love to hear God's voice, don't we? We hear his voice in our consciences, we hear God's voice in and through creation and providence, and we hear God's voice loudest and clearest in his word. We love to hear God's voice more than any other voice. That's why it pains us when others ignore or try to muffle or silence his voice with their loud voices. *How can we amplify God's voice over every other voice?* In Psalm 29, David agonizes over this and helps us turn our pain into praise.

Great People Avoid God's Voice 29:1–2

"Ascribe to the LORD, O heavenly beings" (29:1). Who is David addressing here? It sounds like angels, doesn't it? But why would David urge angels to praise God? They do that anyway. The Hebrew is literally "sons of God," or "sons of the mighty" a phrase sometimes used in the Bible to describe earthly rulers.[1]

What does David tell these powerful men to do? "Ascribe to the LORD glory and strength. Ascribe to the LORD the glory due his name; worship the LORD in the splendor of holiness" (29:1–2). David urges these leaders to openly and vocally credit the Lord

---

1   Some believe this phrase refers to angels. See Calvin's commentary on Psalm 29 for his explanation of why "sons of God" refers to earthly rulers. John Calvin, *Commentary on the Book of Psalms*, vol. 1, trans. James Anderson, Christian Classics Ethereal Library (Grand Rapids, MI: Baker, 1989), https://www.ccel.org/ccel/calvin /calcom08.xxxv.i.html.

with glory and strength. Yet, all he hears back is silence. For all the words these mighty men speak every day, they never say, "Glory to God."

Our lives say either "Glory to God" or "Glory to me."

"What should we do when the great avoid God's voice?"
We amplify God's voice.

God's People Amplify God's Voice 29:3–11

Though the great ignore and avoid God's voice, God's people identify and amplify it. David used two amplifiers. The first was God's providence as he spoke through a thunderstorm. Just as meteorologists name hurricanes, the psalmist also named this storm: "The voice of the LORD." David refers to "the voice of the LORD" seven times and mentions God's name almost twenty times.

God's voice shakes massive mountains to the core (29:6). God's voice divides flames of lightning into innumerable jagged forks (29:7). God's voice fills uninhabitable deserts (29:8). God's voice panics the animals (29:9). God's voice strips the forests bare (29:9). What a noise! What a voice!

The second amplifier was God's people. The people in the palace are deaf to God's voice, but the people in the church amplify it: "In his temple all cry, 'Glory!'" (29:9). They hear God's voice in the storm saying, "Glory to God!" and they echo back, "Glory to God." Seven voices of the Lord prompt multiple voices of believers acting as multiple amplifiers. "The LORD sits enthroned over the flood; the LORD sits enthroned as king forever. May the LORD give strength to his people! May the LORD bless his people with peace!" (29:10–11). God's people don't seek and speak of their own glory and honor. They pivot from earth to heaven, from people to God, and shout, "Glory to God!"

Be one of God's amplifiers.

Changing Our Story with God's Story

When other voices crowd in and threaten to muffle God's voice in our lives, in the church, and in the world, we can turn up the divine volume by praying to God and praising him.

In the New Testament, Jesus got glory from his people—not by raising storms but by calming them (Mark 4:35–41). But the end result was the same: glory to God. "Who then is this, that even the wind and the sea obey him?" (4:41).

Summary: How can we amplify God's voice over every other voice? *Use providence and praise to amplify God's voice to unavoidable decibels.*

Question: How will you amplify God's voice today so that others cannot avoid hearing it?

Prayer: Glorious God, increase your glory in the world by increasing your voice in the world and in the church.

A health loss can be a heart profit.

30

The Blessings of Sickness

PSALM 30

Disease hunts us and sickness stalks us. As soon as we are born—and even when we are still in our mother's womb—death tracks us and tries to attack us. We use every means available to defend ourselves and defeat this deadly foe: diet, exercise, medicine, surgery, and so on. But, one by one, we succumb to sickness, disease, and eventually death.

Sickness, though, need not be only a curse and a loss. With God's blessing, it can also be a time of blessing and gain. *How can we turn sickness from a pain and loss into a comfort and profit?* In Psalm 30, David shows us the blessings of sickness by using sickness as a reason to pray and praise.

Sickness Blesses Us with Prayer 30:2, 8–10

What's the first thing you do when illness strikes? Visit the pharmacy? Call the doctor? The first thing David did was pray: "O LORD my God, I cried to you for help, and you have healed me" (30:2). We get more details of his prayer later in the psalm: "To you, O LORD, I cry, and to the Lord I plead for mercy: 'What profit is there in my death, if I go down to the pit? Will the dust praise you? Will it tell of your faithfulness? Hear, O LORD, and be merciful to me! O LORD, be my helper!'" (30:8–10). Sickness accelerated and intensified David's supplication. He used his physical weakness to grow spiritual strength.

A health loss can be a heart profit.

"What other benefits are found in physical illness?"
The blessing of praise.

Sickness Blesses Us with Praise 30: 1–12

This psalm is a song of praise to the God who heals. It begins with praise: "I will extol you, O Lord, for you have drawn me up and have not let my foes rejoice over me" (30:1).

It goes on in praise: "Sing praises to the Lord, O you his saints, and give thanks to his holy name. For his anger is but for a moment, and his favor is for a lifetime. Weeping may tarry for the night, but joy comes with the morning" (30:4–5).

And it ends with praise: "You have turned for me my mourning into dancing; you have loosed my sackcloth and clothed me with gladness, that my glory may sing your praise and not be silent. O Lord my God, I will give thanks to you forever!" (30:11–12).

"But," you might protest, "David praised God because God answered his prayer with healing. I'm praying, yet I'm still sick. How do I praise?"

In present sickness we can praise God for past healings. In present sickness, we can also praise God for future healing. Whether we will be healed from this sickness while we live is unknown. What we do know is that we will be healed from all sickness when we die. As Christians enter heaven, they sing: "You have turned for me my mourning into dancing; you have loosed my sackcloth and clothed me with gladness, that my glory may sing your praise and not be silent. O Lord my God, I will give thanks to you forever!" (30:11–12). So why not practice that song now?

Death heals every disease.

Changing Our Story with God's Story

As you sing this song, think beyond your own suffering to the suffering of Christ that secured your ultimate healing. Think of Jesus singing this psalm in his suffering. He used his suffering to pray and praise. I see him emerging from the tomb on Easter Sunday morning, and I hear this song on his lips. Sing it from that perspective, and you'll turn your sickness into prayer and praise.

Summary: How can you turn sickness from a pain and loss into a comfort and profit? *Use sickness as a reason to pray and praise and you'll get comfort and profit.*

Question: How has this psalm changed the way you view disease and death? Can you help others change their perspective with this psalm?

Prayer: Divine Doctor, you are in charge of all sickness, disease, and death. Heal me physically or use my physical sickness to heal me spiritually and be a means of healing to others.

God's kindness
is our courage.

Hear
God's Story

Change
Your Story

Tell
the Story

Change
Others' Stories

31

God's Goodness versus People's Badness

PSALM 31

Abby worked hard at her studies and sports and loved the social side of high school. She had a growing friend group and a BFF named Chloe. Life was good.

Until it wasn't.

One day, as soon as she got on the school bus, Abby knew something was different. Someone was in her seat talking to Chloe, and neither of them looked up. As she searched for a spare seat, everyone looked away. "What's going on?" she wondered.

Throughout the day, she noticed groups of people whispering and looking at her. Her friend group excluded her, and Chloe avoided her. After lunch, she saw a note taped to her locker. As she got closer, she was horrified. "Slut!" What? She tore the note off and slumped to the floor in tears. *"How will I ever recover from this terrible slander?"*

She felt an arm on her shoulder and looked up through her tears to see Eva, one of the older girls. "I'm so sorry, Abby. The same thing happened to me last year. I know you don't deserve that reputation. Neither did I, but someone decided to start and spread lies. It's so evil, but I learned a big lesson from it all: God's goodness is bigger and better than people's badness." Eva learned that from Psalm 31.

People's Badness Is Big 31:1–18

Abby and Eva met after school to chat. Eva shared with Abby how God had used Psalm 31 to help her when people slandered her. They read a verse each, noticing how people's badness made the psalmist turn to God's goodness (31:1–8). Abby found verses 9–18 especially comforting because she identified with what the psalmist was feeling when he was slandered. She felt as though David and God were saying to her, "We feel your pain."

In this internet and social media age, very few of us escape misrepresentation and slander. I've certainly endured my unfair share of it. It's tempting to retaliate, or to hide away and become less of a target. Instead of lashing out or checking out, we need to cry out to God for his comfort.

God's compassion is our comfort.

"Compassion in suffering is great, but we also need courage to live."
We get that from God's almighty goodness.

God's Goodness Is Bigger 31:19–24

Verse 19 stunned Abby: "Oh, how abundant is your goodness, which you have stored up for those who fear you and worked for those who take refuge in you, in the sight of the children of mankind!" In the midst of so much human badness, God's overflowing goodness is a beautiful sight and welcome relief. Abby could join heartily in verse 21: "Blessed be the Lord, for he has wondrously shown his steadfast love to me when I was in a besieged city." And then, what a climax at the end: "Love the Lord, all you his saints! The Lord preserves the faithful but abundantly repays the one who acts in pride. Be strong, and let your heart take courage, all you who wait for the Lord!" (31:23–24).

God's kindness is our courage.

Changing Our Story with God's Story

Eva said, "Abby, you've found comfort and courage by taking these words as your own. But we can go further; we can turn these words into the highest worship when we hear them as spoken by Jesus when his holy character was slandered."

God's goodness enveloped them as the two girls reread the psalm from Jesus's viewpoint. The slander against Abby took many weeks to fade, but every time Abby felt the pain of people's badness, she turned to God and whispered, "Oh, how abundant is your goodness!"

Summary: How will I ever recover from terrible slander? *Remember that God's goodness is bigger and better than people's badness.*

Question: How will knowing this psalm change the way you handle future slanders compared to how you handled past slanders?

Prayer: Good, Good Father, thank you for your superabounding kindness in the midst of people's badness.

The fullest forgiveness is the highest happiness.

32

The Greatest Happiness

PSALM 32

What brings you the most happiness? Do you have something in mind? Good. Now, let me ask you some questions about this source of your greatest happiness. Is it deep, or superficial? Is it permanent, or temporary? Is it holy, or sinful? Is it helpful, or harmful? Is it free, or expensive? Is it available, or often unavailable? Is it easily shared with others, or does it make you selfish?

Did you mainly answer with the second of all these alternatives? Is the source of your greatest happiness superficial, temporary, sinful, harmful, expensive, unavailable, and selfish? How would you like a happiness that ticks all the other boxes? A happiness that is deep, permanent, holy, helpful, free, available, and shared with others? *Where can we find the best happiness?* Let's join David as he finds it in Psalm 32.

Forgiveness Causes Happiness 32:1-2

David is euphoric, excited, elated, and exhilarated. Why? Did he win the lottery? Did he get a promotion? Did he graduate? Did he win the championship? No, none of the above. He was forgiven. That's it? That's everything!

Listen to the joy and jubilation in these words: "Blessed is the one whose transgression is forgiven, whose sin is covered. Blessed is the man against whom the Lord counts no iniquity, and in whose spirit there is no deceit" (32:1-2). Blessed! Blessed! Happy! Happy!

My sin is completely covered. God's red blood paints over my every dark stain. "Blessed is the one whose transgression is forgiven, whose sin is covered." My sin-count is zero. God's pressed AC ("All Clear") on his sin-calculator. "Blessed is the man against whom the LORD counts no iniquity."

This was possible even in the Old Testament as saints looked forward in faith to the Messiah's sacrifice, just as it is possible for us as we look back in faith to the same sacrifice.

The fullest forgiveness is the highest happiness.

"How do I get this forgiveness?"
It comes from God via confession.

Forgiveness Comes through Confession 32:3–5

David wasn't always so happy: "For when I kept silent, my bones wasted away through my groaning all day long. For day and night your hand was heavy upon me; my strength was dried up as by the heat of summer" (32:3–4). Misery and mourning! Sadness and sorrow!

How did he get into this state? By staying silent. How did he get out of it? By speaking. When David was silent about his sin, he was miserable. But when he started speaking to God about it, he enjoyed forgiveness: "I acknowledged my sin to you, and I did not cover my iniquity; I said, 'I will confess my transgressions to the LORD,' and you forgave the iniquity of my sin" (32:5).

Sin had shut David's mouth before God and others. But once he spoke to God in confession, he started speaking to others about confession.

Sin muzzles us, but confession frees us.

Changing Our Story with God's Story

Confession, forgiveness, happiness. Confession, forgiveness, happiness. That's the constant cycle of the Christian life. This is why David calls us to join him in his exuberant praise: "Therefore let everyone who is godly offer prayer to you at a time when you may be found; surely in the rush of great waters, they shall not reach him. You are a hiding place for me; you preserve me from trouble; you surround me with shouts of deliverance" (32:6–7). David invites us to follow his example rather than to stubbornly resist like a donkey (32:8–9), and he promises willing confessors that they will be surrounded by God's steadfast love (32:10). No wonder he ends on the same joyful chord that he began with: "Be glad in the Lord, and rejoice, O righteous, and shout for joy, all you upright in heart!" (32:11).

Summary: Where can I find the greatest happiness? *Find your greatest happiness in Christ's forgiveness through your confession.*

Question: What sin can you confess today to increase your happiness today?

Prayer: Forgiver of Sin, I confess my sins to you to get deep, permanent, holy, helpful, free, available, and shared happiness.

God loves to look
at those who look
at his love.

33

God's Steadfast Love in a World of Hate

PSALM 33

Almost daily we read headlines about hatred in America that threatens to destroy our society. Whatever country we live in, division and aggression are depressing and frightening, aren't they? *How can we find love and joy in a world of hate and anger?*

The psalmist seems to have found the answer. He sings, "Shout for joy in the Lord, O you righteous! Praise befits the upright. Give thanks to the Lord with the lyre; make melody to him with the harp of ten strings! Sing to him a new song; play skillfully on the strings, with loud shouts" (33:1–3). How? Why? "The earth is full of the steadfast love of the Lord" (33:5), he answers, and then opens our eyes to see and enjoy God's steadfast love in a world of hate.

See God's Steadfast Love in His Steadfast Creation 33:6–9

Stop and study what the Lord has made. We see his big and powerful love in *what* he created: the planets, the stars, and the oceans (33:6–7). We see his big and powerful love in *why* he created: he made the world to make us worship (33:8). We see his big and powerful love in *how* he created: "He spoke, and it came to be; he commanded, and it stood firm" (33:9). Just as the world is full of God's glory, it is also full of his steadfast love. Does that not fill us with awe?

God made an awesome world to make an awe-filled people.

"God made the world, but is he in control of it?"
Yes, perfectly.

See God's Steadfast Love in His Steadfast Providence 33:10–16

Here's today's news: "The LORD brings the counsel of the nations to nothing; he frustrates the plans of the peoples. The counsel of the LORD stands forever, the plans of his heart to all generations. Blessed is the nation whose God is the LORD, the people whom he has chosen as his heritage!" (33:10–12).

That doesn't sound like CNN or Fox News, does it? That's because journalists tell us what they see, but this psalm tells us what God sees. Let God's headlines soothe you: "The LORD looks down from heaven; he sees all the children of man; from where he sits enthroned he looks out on all the inhabitants of the earth, he who fashions the hearts of them all and observes all their deeds. The king is not saved by his great army; a warrior is not delivered by his great strength" (33:13–16).

God's love overrules human hate.

"God's steadfast love makes the world and rules the world,
but can it save the world?" It can save all who want to be saved.

See God's Steadfast Love in His Steadfast Salvation 33:18–22

God doesn't have his eye only on our leaders: "Behold, the eye of the LORD is on those who fear him, on those who hope in his steadfast love" (33:18). God's steadfast love for his people is a steadfast gaze on his people. He never takes his loving eye off them. Therefore, we never take our loving eyes off him: "Our soul waits for the LORD; he is our help and our shield. For our heart is glad in him, because we trust in his holy name" (33:20–21).

God loves to look at those who look at his love.

Changing Our Story with God's Story

After seeing God's steadfast love in his steadfast creation, his steadfast providence, and his steadfast salvation, our heart bursts with: "Let your steadfast love, O LORD, be upon us, even as we hope in you" (33:22).

Summary: How can we find love and joy in a world of hate and anger? *Enjoy God's steadfast love in a world of horrible hate by seeing his steadfast creation, providence, and salvation.*

Question: What do you need to see more of? God's steadfast love in his steadfast creation, in his steadfast providence, or in his steadfast salvation?

Prayer: Steadfast God, give me steadfast enjoyment of your steadfast love in creation, providence, and salvation.

God doesn't give us everything; he gives us every good thing.

34

What Is the Good Life?

PSALM 34

"What is the good life?" Socrates, Aristotle, and many other philosophers have attempted to answer this question through the centuries. A Google search found twenty songs with that title, as well as fourteen albums, seven books, five films, and three TV series. We've all asked the question, haven't we? What would be my dream life? *What is the good life, and how do I find it?*

At the heart of this question is a confession that we haven't found the good life, that good is missing from our lives. It's saying, "I am not good, and my life is not good." But it's also a cry for good. So, what is the good life? And how do I get it? God answers through Psalm 34.

God Is Good 34:1–8

We find David in a good mood. He's praising God and calling us to join him in making God big and high (34:1–3). Why? Because when he was filled with bad fears and surrounded by bad foes, God delivered him from both (34:4–7). He therefore exclaims, "Oh, taste and see that the LORD is good! Blessed is the man who takes refuge in him!" (34:8). As the only one who is good and the only source of all good, God is the ultimate answer to the good-life question.

The good-life question has a good-God answer.

"How do I get God's goodness into my life?"
You get it when God gives it.

God Gives Good 34:10

David takes us to the jungle and points out that "the young lions suffer want and hunger; but those who seek the Lord lack no good thing" (34:10). God gives good to those who lack it. This doesn't mean that God gives us everything. No, it means he gives us every good thing. He will not give us what will ultimately harm us, but only what will do us good. Thankfully, God knows the difference even when we don't.

God doesn't give us everything;
he gives us every good thing.

"I'm grateful for getting good, but how do I give good and be good too?" Our good God teaches how to give good and be good.

God Makes Good 34:11–22

We've tasted good in God, and we've received good from God, but how do we live a good life for God? "Come, O children, listen to me; I will teach you the fear of the Lord. What man is there who desires life and loves many days, that he may see good?" (34:11–13). This answer involves both turning from bad and doing good: "Keep your tongue from evil and your lips from speaking deceit. Turn away from evil and do good; seek peace and pursue it" (34:13–14). Do good even to those who want to do us bad, and God will do even greater good to you, for you, and through you (34:15–22).

God makes us live good for a good life.

Changing Our Story with God's Story

No matter how good a life we live in this world, it is never perfectly good and we are never perfectly good. As Jesus said, "No one is good except God alone" (Mark 10:18). No matter how hard we try, because of our sin we will never be perfectly good or live a perfectly good life. The only one who did live a perfectly good life was Jesus. He offers us his good life to replace our bad life before God. And if we accept, we know that our bad lives on earth will be followed by perfectly good lives in heaven. No one in heaven is asking, "Who will show us any good?"

Summary: What is the good life, and how do I find it? *Seek the good life in our good God, and he will make you good and use you for good.*

Question: What other ways do you try to find the good life, and how have they succeeded?

Prayer: Good God, you alone are good, you alone give good, and you alone will make good. Therefore, help me to find the good life in you.

God is the equalizer, so we're not to be vigilantes.

35

The Equalizer

PSALM 35

In my early twenties, I enjoyed watching a TV series called *The Equalizer*. A retired intelligence agent used the skills from his former career to exact justice on behalf of innocent victims of evil. The show eventually got too violent for me, and I had to turn it off (modern versions of the show are even worse). However, there's something appealing about the idea of an equalizer. We long to see evil punished and the innocent vindicated. So, *where can we find true justice when injustice is triumphing?* That's where Psalm 35 helps us.

Persecutors Drive Us to God 35:1–3

David suffered long and hard at the hands of Saul, and therefore prayed long and hard for the hand of God to intervene: "Contend, O Lord, with those who contend with me; fight against those who fight against me! Take hold of shield and buckler and rise for my help! Draw the spear and javelin against my pursuers! Say to my soul, 'I am your salvation!'" (35:1–3). Instead of driving David from God, unjust enemies drove him to God.

Hatred from enemies deepens love for God.

"But surely I have to fight back?"
No, God will fight back for you.

Persecutors Will Be Punished by God 35:4–14

David trusted God to be the equalizer and therefore prayed for that: "Let them be put to shame and dishonor who seek after my life! Let them be turned back and disappointed who devise evil against me! Let them be like chaff before the wind, with the angel of the Lord driving them away!" (35:4–5). David rejected personal retaliation but embraced divine retribution.

While praying for God's justice against his enemies, David continued to love his enemies on a personal level: "But I, when they were sick—I wore sackcloth; I afflicted myself with fasting; I prayed with head bowed on my chest. I went about as though I grieved for my friend or my brother; as one who laments his mother, I bowed down in mourning" (35:13–14). David was not vindictive. While longing for God's justice, he also longed for his enemies' salvation.

God is the equalizer, so we're not to be vigilantes.

"If I must leave vindication to God, what do I do instead?"
Sing praises to God.

Persecutors Lead Us to Praise God 35:9–10, 27–28

Meting out justice to persecutors was God's job; praising God was David's job. Instead of fighting back, he fights to praise God. Whether or not David wins, God wins praise through David's singing bones: "My soul will rejoice in the Lord, exulting in his salvation. All my bones shall say, 'O Lord, who is like you, delivering the poor from him who is too strong for him, the poor and needy from him who robs him?'" (35:9–10). He battled back to this theme at the end of the psalm: "Let those who delight in my righteousness shout for joy and be glad and say evermore, 'Great is the Lord, who delights in the welfare of his servant'" (35:27–28).

When enemies break our bones,
our bones break out in praise.

Changing Our Story with God's Story

When everything is so unequal, we love an equalizer. What a comfort to know that all injustices will one day be put right by our just and holy God!

But Jesus took justice a step further. He took the just punishment of evildoers on himself in order to save evildoers. He suffered God's justice to save sinners from God's justice: "For Christ also suffered once for sins, the righteous for the unrighteous, that he might bring us to God" (1 Pet. 3:18). Now that's an equalizer we all need.

Summary: Where can we find true justice when injustice is triumphing? *When enemies attack, turn to (not into) the equalizer.*

Question: How will this change the way you deal with your enemies?

Prayer: Just God, you are the judge of all, and you will act justly. I therefore run to you with the injustices I suffer and trust you with justice as I praise your justice.

Don't assume God's love; ask for it.

 Hear God's Story | Change Your Story | Tell the Story | Change Others' Stories

36

The Media's Business Model

PSALM 36

The media's business model used to focus on information, but now it focuses on provocation. Whether we're talking about the left or the right, more money is poured into provoking us than informing us. Notice how many reports, columns, panels, and so on are designed to provoke anger and anxiety. Why? Because the more anger and anxiety they can produce, the more people will watch, which results in more advertising dollars. Harmful feelings are more profitable than helpful facts.

So, how do we avoid being changed for the worse by the media? Let's follow David in Psalm 36 as he switches off the human anger and anxiety channel and switches over to the divine love and life channel. His example instructs us to switch channels in order to switch feelings.

God's Love Is Immeasurable 36:3-5

Although David didn't have Fox News or CNN, the powerful and influential still used words to terrify others: "The words of his mouth are trouble and deceit; he has ceased to act wisely and do good. He plots trouble while on his bed; he sets himself in a way that is not good; he does not reject evil" (36:3-4).

So David switched from the big anger channel to the big love channel: "Your steadfast love, O LORD, extends to the heavens" (36:5). How big is God's love? As big as the universe. The distance between earth and the edge of the observable universe is 46 billion light years.

In other words, it would take light, traveling at 300,000 miles per second, 46 billion years to travel from earth to the edge of the observable universe. "Your steadfast love, O Lord, extends to the heavens" (36:5). In this sense alone, we can say God's love is universal.

God's love is spatially universal, but not savingly universal.

"God's love is bigger than I can imagine, but is it better than I can imagine?" Far better. It's beyond imagination.

God's Love Is Invaluable 36:7–9

If you really loved your wife, you wouldn't give her a diamond—you'd give her a Tanzanite. Tanzanite, discovered in 1967, is found only in northern Tanzania, and it is the world's most valuable gemstone. In fact, diamonds place a lowly ninth in the top ten of valuable gemstones.

But there's something even more valuable than Tanzanite: God's love. David exclaims, "How precious is your steadfast love, O God!" (36:7). How valuable is it? It's so valuable that it cannot be valued. It's invaluable. So, instead of putting a figure on God's love, David meditates on metaphors of it: "The children of mankind take refuge in the shadow of your wings. They feast on the abundance of your house, and you give them drink from the river of your delights. For with you is the fountain of life; in your light do we see light" (36:7–9).

Picture God's love to profit from God's love.

"How do I get this love?"
Desire it.

God's Love Is Desirable 36:10

Given that God's love is immeasurable and invaluable, it's no wonder that David prays for more of it: "Oh, continue your steadfast love to those who know you" (36:10). He doesn't want God's love to be a distant memory, but a living reality. He doesn't take it for granted, but prays for it.

Don't assume God's love; ask for it.

Changing Our Story with God's Story

Can you imagine how much happier we'd be if we watched the love channel rather than the hate channel? Anger and anxiety would drain away and love and life would fill us. We would love God and people more. There's no brighter, better picture of God's love than the cross of Christ. There we see clearly that God's love is immeasurable, invaluable, and desirable.

Summary: So, how do I avoid being changed for the worse by the media's channels? *Switch from the human anger channel to the divine love channel to switch your heart feelings for the better.*

Question: What will you now change about your media habits?

Prayer: God of Love, switch me to your best channel to switch my feelings for the better.

God not only rules us, he also reasons with us.

Hear
God's Story

Change
Your Story

Tell
the Story

Change
Others' Stories

37

Rest for Rioters

PSALM 37

From time to time, riots erupt in American society. Usually, they are fueled by a seething sense of injustice that boils over in sinful and destructive fury.

Whether rioters are right or wrong in their sense of injustice, I understand the anger that such feelings produce. I too have been the victim of injustice, and I too have lashed out at the perpetrators, not with my fists but with my tongue.

Most of us will get to that boiling point at some point in our lives. We will be provoked with injustice and be tempted to act out in verbal or physical violence. *How can we calm our feelings of injustice and the destructive anger it produces?* Let's soothe our souls with Psalm 37.

Use God's Rules to Calm the Riot 37:1–8

A sense of injustice at the hands of the wicked penetrated deep into David's heart, provoking both pain and sin. He counseled and cautioned himself as he sensed sinful feelings and thoughts mixing into a toxic brew.

When he saw envy and anxiety seeding, he counseled himself: "Fret not yourself because of evildoers; be not envious of wrongdoers!" (37:1). When he saw distrust and evil stirring in himself, he counseled himself: "Trust in the Lord, and do good" (37:3). When he sensed spiritual cooling, he counseled himself: "Delight yourself in the Lord" (37:4). When he thought of taking the law into his own hands, he counseled himself: "Commit your way to the Lord; trust in him, and he will act" (37:5). When he felt anger rising, he counseled himself: "Refrain from anger, and forsake wrath! Fret not yourself; it tends only to evil" (37:8). Read through the psalm and see how David used God's commands to calm the insurrection from within.

God's commands cause inner calm.

"Rules help me, but what about when that's not enough?"
God reasons with us too.

Use God's Reasons to Calm the Riot 37:2–16

Sometimes faith must act upon the bare commands of God. But, more commonly, God supplies reasons for his commands. He tells us not only what to do, but why to do it. That's what we see in Psalm 37 as David tamps down his inner riot not only with God's rules but also with God's reasons. Don't envy the wicked, because "they will soon fade like the grass and wither like the green herb" (37:2). Delight in God, because "he will give you the desires of your heart" (37:4). Commit your case to the Lord, because "he will bring forth your righteousness as the light, and your justice as the noonday" (37:6). Forsake anger, because "the evildoers shall be cut off, but those who wait for the Lord shall inherit the land" (37:9). Don't envy the prosperity of the wicked, because "better is the little that the righteous has than the abundance of many wicked" (37:16). Again, go through the psalm and see how David not only commands his inner rioters but also reasons with them.

God not only rules us, he also reasons with us.

Changing Our Story with God's Story

I've often used this psalm to restore law and order in my heart. I need both God's rules and God's reasons to quell the dangerous rioters in my heart, mind, and mouth. Like David, I often fail at this, but then I worship my Savior, Jesus Christ, who used this psalm perfectly when he was the innocent victim of a riot from hell; he perfectly submitted to it for my salvation (1 Pet. 2:21–24).

Summary: How can we calm our feelings of injustice and the destructive anger it produces? *We can calm our inner riot with God's rules and God's reasons.*

Question: What boils your temper, and how can you use God's rules and reasons to lower the temperature of your temper?

Prayer: Calm God, give me your calm in my soul by soothing me with your rules and your reasons.

Discipline hurts to heal.

38

God's Correction and Our Confession

PSALM 38

Parenting has many pleasures and some pains. The greatest pain might be disciplining our children. We love our kids, and it pains us to pain them. But we know that, sometimes, discipline is the only way to correct them and thereby prevent far worse pain for them in the future. It's still really hard, but we know the Bible commands it and warns us of far worse consequences if we don't (e.g., Prov. 13:18; 19:18).

As our Father, God has to discipline us. It gives him no pleasure, but he loves us too much to allow us to continue sinning with no correction. *How should we respond to God's fatherly correction?* Let's see what David did in Psalm 38, when he was flinching under the pain of God's correction.

God Will Correct Sin 38:1–12

The first two verses leave us in no doubt about what was happening: "O Lord, rebuke me not in your anger, nor discipline me in your wrath! For your arrows have sunk into me, and your hand has come down on me" (38:1–2). God's discipline pained David in three ways—physically, emotionally, and relationally.

First, there was physical pain: "There is no soundness in my flesh because of your indignation; there is no health in my bones because of my sin. For my iniquities have gone over my head; like a heavy burden, they are too heavy for me. My wounds stink and fester because of my foolishness, I am utterly bowed down and prostrate; all the day I go about mourning. For my sides are filled with burning, and there is no soundness in my flesh" (38:3–7).

Second, there was emotional pain: "I am feeble and crushed; I groan because of the tumult of my heart. O Lord, all my longing is before you; my sighing is not hidden from you. My heart throbs; my strength fails me, and the light of my eyes—it also has gone from me" (38:8–10).

Third, there was relational pain. His friends ran from him: "My friends and companions stand aloof from my plague, and my nearest kin stand far off" (38:11). His enemies ran after him: "Those who seek my life lay their snares; those who seek my hurt speak of ruin and meditate treachery all day long" (38:12).

David was focused on his physical, emotional, and relational pain, but God was focused on spiritual correction.

Discipline hurts to heal.

"I understand the need for correction, but how do I get healing?"
By confession.

We Must Confess Sin 38:15–22

It took David a while to get there, but eventually he turned to God in repentance. Complaining drove him from God, but confessing brought him to God: "But for you, O Lord, do I wait; it is you, O Lord my God, who will answer" (38:15); "I confess my iniquity; I am sorry for my sin" (38:18); "I follow after good" (38:20). God's correction prompted godly confession and produced godly character. Sin says, "I don't fear God's presence." Repentance says, "I fear God's absence." "Do not forsake me, O Lord! O my God, be not far from me! Make haste to help me, O Lord, my salvation!" (38:21–22).

God's correction is painful,
but God's desertion is more agonizing.

Changing Our Story with God's Story

Our flesh feels the pain of God's correction, but our faith feels God's love in it. So let's follow David's example by turning the pain of correction into godly character via godly confession. God takes no pleasure in our discipline, but he takes massive pleasure in our sanctification. Only God's perfect Son, Jesus, needed no correction, had no sin to confess, and possessed a perfectly holy character. God loves his Son and us so much that he changes his sons and daughters to be like him (Rom. 8:29; Eph. 1:5).

Summary: How should we respond to God's fatherly correction? *Respond to God's correction with godly confession and godly character.*

Question: How is God correcting you? What have you to confess? What character is God wanting to produce in you?

Prayer: My Loving Father, thank you for your discipline. Use it to replace rotten fruit with good fruit, and my bad with your good. Train me to resist sin so that I will be spared more discipline.

Breathe better to live better.

39

A New Breathing Exercise

PSALM 39

Breath: The New Science of a Lost Art was published in May 2020 and quickly became a *New York Times* bestseller. Chapter 1 is titled "The Worst Breathers in the Animal Kingdom." That's us. The author, James Nestor, argues that poor breathing is harming us. He therefore teaches us to breathe better to be better.

The author of Psalm 39 also wants us to breathe better to be better. He teaches us a simple breathing exercise that will help us not only be better but die better. *How can breathing better help us die better?*

Life Is a Short Breath 39:1–6

Here's the exercise: breathe in, breathe out. That's it. Pretty simple, isn't it? "But I do that all day and all night already. What's different?" What's different is what you think about while doing it. Here's a simple thought to pair with a simple breath: "Surely all mankind stands as a mere breath!" (39:5). David's point is that we are as brief as a breath.

It looks as though David penned this psalm at the funeral of a loved one. He was struggling to accept the loss and didn't want to say anything that would damage his witness before the world (39:1–3). Eventually, though, he could no longer hold his tongue, and he cried "O LORD, make me know my end and what is the measure of my days; let me know how fleeting I am! Behold, you have made my days a few handbreadths, and my lifetime is as nothing before you. Surely all mankind stands as a mere breath! *Selah*. Surely a man goes about as a shadow! Surely for nothing they are in turmoil; man heaps up wealth and does not know who will gather!" (39:4–6). The more we realize how short life is, the more we'll treasure life and use it better.

Breathe better to live better.

"But if life is so brief, I need help to die."
Think about your last breath in order to help you to die better.

Life Has a Last Breath 39:11–13

While thinking that life is a breath, David anticipates his last life breath. He turns from the breathless body of his loved one and sees more painful loss in his future. He knows he'll be back in this grave-yard with more breathless loved ones and exclaims again, "Surely all mankind is a mere breath!" (39:11). As David breathes in and out, it dawns on him that he will one day breathe out and never breathe in again. He will have a last breath. "I am a sojourner with you, a guest, like all my fathers. Look away from me, that I may smile again, before I depart and am no more!" (39:12–13).

As in Psalm 38, David senses that God is disciplining him, this time through the loss of loved ones. He asks that God might pause this pain so that he can have one last smile before drawing his last breath.

Breathe better to die better.

Changing Our Story with God's Story

We can't think about our own breathing without thinking about Jesus's breathing. The eternal one, who gave "to all mankind life and breath and everything" (Acts 17:25), took a pair of lungs. He began to breathe and cry in Bethlehem and all too soon "uttered a loud cry and breathed his last" on Calvary (Mark 15:37). He breathed his last breath so that we could live after our last breath. He breathed again in the tomb so that we could breathe again in heaven.

Summary: How can breathing better help me to die better? *Think about your life as a breath and think about your last breath of life in order to live better and die better.*

Question: How can you use your breath as a teacher? What breathing exercises can you do to help you in spiritual exercise?

Prayer: Giver of Breath, thank you for giving me breath to live for you. Help me to breathe every breath for you so that when I no longer breathe, I will be with you.

Refocus on salvation to revive your songs.

40

A Solution for Election Problems

PSALM 40

I've met many Christians who struggle with difficult doctrines, particularly the doctrine of election. Many question whether they are part of God's elect, whether God had truly chosen them to be saved. The concern can become an obsession, dominating believers' lives so much that it squeezes out every other truth. The preoccupation with the doctrine of election can silence praise, paralyze service, and hinder prayers.

The devil loves when this happens. He wants us to focus on anything other than salvation. He'll even use a doctrine related to salvation to keep us from salvation. *How can we keep salvation central and election secondary?* Psalm 40 reminds us to always keep salvation primary and everything else secondary.

Salvation Revives Our Songs 40:1–3

David goes back to where God first found him, crying out as he sank deeper and deeper into a slimy pit (40:1). God intervened in powerful mercy: "He drew me up from the pit of destruction, out of the miry bog, and set my feet upon a rock, making my steps secure" (40:2). The result? Revived worship: "He put a new song in my mouth, a song of praise to our God. Many will see and fear, and put their trust in the LORD" (40:3).

Refocus on salvation to revive your songs.

"So, I'm singing again, but what about serving again?"
Salvation is the best fuel for that too.

Salvation Resurrects Our Service 40:6–10

Refocusing on salvation also resurrected David's service. He re-committed himself to God privately in his heart (40:6–8) and then relaunched his public service (40:9–10). A private closeness to God incited a public witness for God: "I have told the glad news of deliverance in the great congregation; behold, I have not restrained my lips, as you know, O Lord. I have not hidden your deliverance within my heart; I have spoken of your faithfulness and your salvation; I have not concealed your steadfast love and your faithfulness from the great congregation" (40:9–10).

Refocus on salvation to resurrect your service.

"But what about recovering my prayer life?"
Salvation is the savior of our prayer life too.

Salvation Rouses Our Prayers 40:11–17

Refocusing on salvation revived David's songs and resurrected his service. But that doesn't mean he forgot all about the evil and injustice in his society. Not at all. But his refocus did help him put such wickedness in the right place, which is third on his list (40:11–17). He sang first, served second, and sought justice third, primarily by praying. And even then, having prayed for justice, he returned to refocus on salvation at the end of the psalm: "But may all who seek you rejoice and be glad in you; may those who love your salvation say continually, 'Great is the Lord!'" (40:16).

Refocus on salvation to rouse your prayers.

Changing Our Story with God's Story

When I was a seminary professor, I saw men come to the school full of great love for the Savior and for the lost. They were consumed with proclaiming the gospel to unbelievers and sharing the message of salvation with them. But as the years of study took their toll, often their ardor cooled. They got distracted with Greek, Hebrew, church history, exegesis, hermeneutics, and so on. They got taken up with academia, advanced degrees, and internet controversy. Indeed, I must confess, I saw my young self in them. The only way to keep praise, service, and prayer alive is by keeping salvation alive in our souls.

Summary: How can I keep salvation central? *Refocus on salvation to revive your songs, resurrect your service, and rouse your prayers.*

Question: What distracts you from salvation, and how will you fight to keep salvation first so that you praise, serve, and pray with joy?

Prayer: Jesus, thank you for your salvation that changes my whole worldview. Its lens puts everything in the right perspective, proportion, and priority. Give me a laser-focus on your salvation because you are worth my songs, service, and prayers.

We don't deserve mercy, but we beg for mercy.

41

Mercy for the Merciful

PSALM 41

We live in an increasingly merciless society. Make one mistake, and the social media mobs will come for you and cancel you in seconds. There seems to be no forgiveness or second chances. Numerous actors, singers, CEOs, politicians, professors, students, and employees have been cancelled for one misstep, even one from their dim and distant past. Many people walk on eggshells, terrified of saying or doing anything that might turn them into social lepers. Social justice seems to be the most antisocial justice in the world. *How do we keep mercy alive in a merciless world?* In Psalm 41, David directs us to social mercy rooted in divine mercy.

The Merciful Get Mercy 41:1-4

David is on his sick bed. He's feeling so poorly that he fears he's dying. In his weakness, he meditates on God's mercy to him shown through the mercy of others.

As he thinks on God's mercy, he blesses those who have been merciful: "Blessed is the one who considers the poor! In the day of trouble the Lord delivers him; the Lord protects him and keeps him alive; he is called blessed in the land; you do not give him up to the will of his enemies. The Lord sustains him on his sickbed; in his illness you restore him to full health" (41:1–3). As Jesus later put it: "Blessed are the merciful, for they shall receive mercy" (Matt. 5:7).

Neither David nor Jesus taught that we get mercy by earning it. Mercy, by definition, is given to the undeserving, a fact that David recognizes: "As for me, I said, 'O LORD, be gracious to me; heal me, for I have sinned against you!'" (41:4). He confesses that he doesn't deserve mercy, because he is a sinner; he begs for it because he is a sinner.

We don't deserve mercy,
but we beg for mercy.

"The merciful get mercy, but what do the merciless get?"
They get what they deserve.

The Merciless Get Justice 41:5–11

Although David got mercy from some, he got murder from others. They spoke *murderous* words: "My enemies say of me in malice, 'When will he die, and his name perish?'" (41:5). They spoke *hollow* words: "And when one comes to see me, he utters empty words, while his heart gathers iniquity" (41:6). They spoke *slanderous* words: "All who hate me whisper together about me; they imagine the worst for me. They say, 'A deadly thing is poured out on him; he will not rise again from where he lies'" (41:7–8). They spoke *deceptive* words: "Even my close friend in whom I trusted, who ate my bread, has lifted his heel against me" (41:9). David talked of kindness, but people talked of killing.

Having failed to get kindness from many, David turned to the kindness of God: "But you, O LORD, be gracious to me, and raise me up, that I may repay them! By this I know that you delight in me: my enemy will not shout in triumph over me" (41:10–11). God in his kindness will not only raise David up, but will enable him as God's appointed king and judge to execute justice on the merciless and defeat their cruel plans.

Civil justice is a divine mercy.

Changing Our Story with God's Story

Realizing the imperfection of mercy and justice in society, David looked away from his present cruel and unjust world to a kind and righteous world in heaven that will last forever: "But you have upheld me because of my integrity, and set me in your presence forever. Blessed be the LORD, the God of Israel, from everlasting to everlasting!" (41:12–13).

Summary: How do we keep mercy alive in a merciless world? *Be merciful, because the merciful get mercy and the merciless get justice.*

Question: To whom will you show mercy today?

Prayer: Merciful God, be merciful to me so that I may be merciful and administer justice to others.

Self-preaching can cure self-pity.

42

The Art of Preaching to Yourself

PSALM 42

Dr. Martyn Lloyd-Jones, the famous British medical doctor turned preacher, asked: "Have you realized that most of your unhappiness in life is due to the fact that you are listening to yourself instead of talking to yourself?"[1] Our own thoughts—influenced by the world, our sin, or our enemy—can undermine our identity and joy in Christ.

How can we reclaim and rebuild our identity and joy in Christ? Thankfully, Lloyd-Jones didn't just diagnose the disease. When preaching on Psalm 42, he prescribed the medicine of preaching to yourself. Let's reflect on this psalm with the help of this spiritual physician.

Preach Challenging Sermons to Yourself 42:1–11

David challenged himself in this psalm. But first he listed his griefs. He wept over his unsatisfied thirst for God (42:1–2), his dark night of the soul (42:3), and his distant memories of packed and joyful corporate worship (42:4).He doesn't deny his pain; he's honest and open about it.

But David didn't stop there. He challenged himself to change his response to these circumstances. He moved from listening to his

---

1   D. Martyn Lloyd-Jones, *Spiritual Depression: Its Causes and Cures* (Grand Rapids, MI: Zondervan, 2016), 20–21, Kindle.

pain to preaching to his pain: "Why are you cast down, O my soul, and why are you in turmoil within me?" (42:5, 11). As Lloyd-Jones explained:

> The main art in the matter of spiritual living is to know how to handle yourself. You have to take yourself in hand, you have to address yourself, preach to yourself, question yourself. You must say to your soul: "Why are you cast down"—what business have you to be disquieted? You must turn on yourself, upbraid yourself, condemn yourself, exhort yourself, and say to yourself: "Hope thou in God" instead of muttering in this depressed, unhappy way.[2]

In a way, we are all preachers, preaching daily sermons to ourselves. The only question is, What kinds of sermons are we preaching and listening to?

Self-preaching can cure self-pity.

"But sometimes I need comfort more than challenge."
Then preach comforting sermons to yourself.

Preach Comforting Sermons to Yourself 42:6–12

David doesn't stop with convicting challenge, but preaches God-centered hope to himself as well. Twice he exhorts himself, "Hope in God; for I shall again praise him, my salvation and my God" (42:6, 12). Notice how his hope isn't just a shaky "hope-so" but a firm God-centered hope. "My soul is cast down within me; therefore I remember you" (42:7). Dr. Lloyd-Jones put it like this:

> Then you must go on to remind yourself of God, who God is, and what God is and what God has done, and what God has

---

2 Lloyd-Jones, *Spiritual Depression*, 20–21.

pledged Himself to do. Then having that, end on this great note: defy yourself, and defy other people, and defy the devil and the whole world, and say with this man: "I shall yet praise Him, for the help of His countenance, who is also the health of my countenance and my God."[3]

Gospel defiance leads to gospel devotion, and gospel protest leads to gospel praise.

Gospel hope is grounded hope.

Changing Our Story with God's Story

I love the honesty of the Psalms. The authors never put a Band-Aid on their pain, but rather let us see their raw and gory wounds. I love their honesty and transparency. But I also love the way they fight for healing hope, as David did here. Notice that the main ingredient in this hope is salvation: "Hope in God; for I shall again praise him, my salvation and my God" (42:6, 11). Salvation through Christ is our support when everything else is crashing to the ground.

Summary: How can I reclaim and rebuild my identity and joy in Christ? *Preach the gospel to yourself.*

Question: How can you preach the gospel to yourself more?

Prayer: Perfect Preacher, teach me to preach the gospel to myself so that I can reclaim and rebuild my identity and joy in Christ even when the outside world and my inside world are a mess.

---

3   Lloyd-Jones, *Spiritual Depression*, 20–21.

People's lies lower us, but God's light lifts us.

43

We Win!

PSALM 43

It's painful to be lied to and even more painful to be lied about. Even if we haven't been victims of lies personally, all Christians are victims of group slander. Every day, Hollywood, the music industry, the mainstream media, Madison Avenue, and corporations churn out movies, shows, songs, articles, commercials, and company policies that soil, smear, and slander Christians.

Misrepresentations, caricatures, distortions, and outright falsehoods darken our days, hurt our hearts, distance us from God, and dampen our prayers and praise. *How do we get up when lies have got us down?* In Psalm 43, a victim of slanderous lies guides us out of the darkness of the world's lies and into the light of God's truth.

Bring Dark Lies to God 43:1-2

The psalmist did not have skin like a rhinoceros. Lies didn't just bounce off him; they wounded him deeply. But he used people's lies to drive him to the God of truth.

"Vindicate me, O God, and defend my cause against an ungodly people, from the deceitful and unjust man deliver me! For you are the God in whom I take refuge; why have you rejected me? Why do I go about mourning because of the oppression of the enemy?" (43:1-2).

When dark lies darken our lives, we turn on the light of God's truth.

Use the dark lies of people to bring you to the bright truth of God.

"So, I've brought all the lies to God. What now?"
God turns on the light.

Get Light and Truth from God 43:3-5

When we're suffocating in lies, we need the oxygen of truth from the God who is truth. Notice how God's truth moves the psalmist from darkness to light, from distance to communion, from depression to joy, from despair to hope, from complaining to praising, and from condemnation to salvation.

"Send out your light and your truth; let them lead me; let them bring me to your holy hill and to your dwelling! Then I will go to the altar of God, to God my exceeding joy, and I will praise you with the lyre, O God, my God. Why are you cast down, O my soul, and why are you in turmoil within me? Hope in God; for I shall again praise him, my salvation and my God" (43:3-5).

What a starkly beautiful contrast to the opening words of this psalm. From darkness, lies, depression, complaint, despair, and condemnation to light, truth, joy, praise, hope, and salvation. Let's join the psalmist with his vigorous verbs: "Send . . . lead . . . bring . . . go."

People's lies lower us, but God's light lifts us.

Changing Our Story with God's Story

If we feel the hurt and heartbreak of lies, how much more did Jesus, who was the truth? No one was more truthful, yet no one was more lied about. He brought the hurt and heartbreak of lies to his Father and got the healing and happiness of truth from his Father. How many times he must have encouraged his heart with the final victory of truth through salvation that is recorded in Psalm 43. Truth will win, and so will we.

Summary: How do I get up when lies have got me down? *When people's lies get you down, use God's truth to lift you up.*

Question: What lies are getting you down, and what truth can get you up?

Prayer: God of Truth and Light, save me from lies and darkness in the world and in me by sending your light and truth into the darkness and the lies.

We can learn more from waiting than winning.

44

We Lost!

PSALM 44

We all want our children to win, don't we? If they're into sports, we want them to win. That's why we sometimes get demented on the sidelines. But sometimes, despite our best efforts on the bleachers, they lose—and it's not a good feeling for them or us. We do the postmortem on the way home and try to find someone to blame—usually the referees—or a lesson to learn.

Psalm 44 is a postmortem after a serious loss for God's people. Psalm 43 gave us the message "We Win!"; but Psalm 44 says, "We Lost!" It recounts a painful time for the defeated church. *Why does God let us lose, and what can we gain from losing?* Let's hear the psalm's answer.

We Won 44:1–8

The spiritual pathologist begins by reminding the church of her past victories: "O God, we have heard with our ears, our fathers have told us, what deeds you performed in their days, in the days of old" (44:1).

He especially wants to remind the church that it was God who gave them every victory: "For not by their own sword did they win the land, nor did their own arm save them, but your right hand and your arm, and the light of your face, for you delighted in them" (44:3). Therefore, "in God we have boasted continually, and we will give thanks to your name forever" (44:8). Their victories made them boast about God not themselves.

The best believers in God are the best boasters in God.

"But what happens when we lose?"
All is not lost.

We Lost 44:9–22

After piling up all the wins, God's people are now licking their wounds: "But you have rejected us and disgraced us and have not gone out with our armies. You have made us turn back from the foe, and those who hate us have gotten spoil" (44:9–10). We're slaughtered and scattered, mocked and scorned, a laughingstock and a disgrace (44:11–16).

This pathologist usually finds sin to be the root cause of spiritual defeats, but in this case the victim is entirely innocent: "All this has come upon us, though we have not forgotten you, and we have not been false to your covenant. Our heart has not turned back, nor have our steps departed from your way; yet you have broken us in the place of jackals and covered us with the shadow of death" (44:17–19). No one is to blame (44:20–22). Sometimes there is no human explanation for a spiritual loss. It is simply God's sovereignty working out his ultimately good and wise plan.

Faithfulness is no guarantee against failure.

"So, what do we do?"
The hardest thing for humans to do—we wait.

We Wait 44:23–26

The church doesn't give up. The church doesn't replace the manager or blame the referee. No, they wait for God: "Awake! Why are you sleeping, O Lord? Rouse yourself! Do not reject us forever!" (44:23); "Rise up; come to our help! Redeem us for the sake of your steadfast love!" (44:26). The pathologist found no cause of death, but did find a lesson to learn how to wait. Waiting for God is sometimes better than winning through God.

We can learn more from
waiting than winning.

Changing Our Story with God's Story

Can you hear our Savior singing this psalm as he suffered the greatest loss ever but turned it into the greatest victory ever? He did not deserve to lose but suffered our greatest losses so that we could get the greatest win.

Summary: Why does God let us lose, and what can we gain from losing? *Learn from losing to turn losing into winning.*

Question: What have you learned from losing?

Prayer: Winning God, you have never lost and you never will, but help me to use my losses so that I can turn losing into winning.

Christ's love makes the Christian laugh.

45

I Love to Laugh

PSALM 45

Growing up in the United Kingdom, royal weddings were a big deal. The one I remember most was the wedding of Prince Charles and Lady Diana in 1981. A national holiday was declared and all-day street parties around the country celebrated this fairy-tale marriage. Television networks even employed lip-readers to guess what the happy couple were saying to each other. The joy of the day lifted the spirits of the whole nation for months.

Psalm 45 gives us a report on an even happier royal wedding, the marriage of God and his people, Israel, which is a prophetic picture of the marriage between Christ and the Christian. *How do these wedding words bring us joy?*

The Bride Rejoices in Her Bridegroom 45:2–8

Use the bride's words to praise Christ our bridegroom, and feel your joy multiplying.

- You are so handsome: "You are the most handsome of the sons of men" (45:2).
- You are so kind: "Grace is poured upon your lips" (45:2).
- You are so blessed: "God has blessed you forever" (45:2).
- You are so brave: "Gird your sword on your thigh, O mighty one. . . . Your arrows are sharp in the heart of the king's enemies; the peoples fall under you" (45:3–5).
- You are so divine: "Your throne, O God, is forever and ever" (45:6).

- You are so holy. "You have loved righteousness and hated wickedness" (45:7).
- You are so happy: "Your God has anointed you with the oil of gladness beyond your companions" (45:7).
- You are so stunning: "Your robes are all fragrant with myrrh and aloes and cassia" (45:8).

Doesn't saying these words to Christ about Christ make you happy?

Loving leads to laughing.

"I love saying these words to Christ, but does Christ say anything to me?" Listen to this.

The Bridegroom Rejoices in His Bride 45:10–16

Hear Christ's loving words to you in response, and feel your joy multiplying.

- You are so mine: "Hear, O daughter, and consider, and incline your ear: forget your people and your father's house" (45:10).
- You are so desirable: "The king will desire your beauty" (45:11). He especially loves your humility and devotion: "Since he is your lord, bow to him" (45:11).
- You are so rich: "The people of Tyre will seek your favor with gifts, the richest of the people" (45:12).
- You are so glorious: "All glorious is the princess in her chamber" (45:13).
- You are so beautiful: "In many-colored robes she is led to the king . . ." (45:14).
- You are so celebrated: ". . . with her virgin companions following behind her. With joy and gladness they are led along as they enter the palace of the king" (45:14–15).

- You are so fruitful: "In place of your fathers shall be your sons; you will make them princes in all the earth" (45:16).

Yes, these are Christ's loving words to you, believer. Is your joy bubbling over yet?

Christ's love makes the Christian laugh.

Changing Our Story with God's Story

The wedding of Charles and Diana started as a fairy tale, but their marriage ended as a nightmare. This royal marriage between Christ and the Christian is completely different because it's a marriage made in heaven. This marriage cannot be broken on earth, and it will live happily ever after in heaven. That's fact, not a fairy tale. As the bride states in the last verse: "I will cause your name to be remembered in all generations; therefore nations will praise you forever and ever" (45:17).

Summary: How do these wedding words bring joy? *Remember Christ's joyful words about you to revive your joyful worship of Christ.*

Question: If Christ were physically standing before you, what words would you use to describe his beauty to him?

Prayer: Beautiful Savior, thank you for loving me with so much joy. Use your joyful words to revive my joyful words of love about you.

This team of one means one team always wins.

46

A Team of One

PSALM 46

Since coming to America thirteen years ago, I've fallen in love with college football. I still don't understand all of the jargon and every tactic, but I do understand that the best teams need both a great defense and a great offense. One without the other is not a championship team. But when both are in place, the whole team has confidence that they will have a winning season.

What can give us confidence in the future victory of the church? Psalm 46 describes the church's awesome defense and offense. It's God. He is our defense and offense. He is a team of one that gives us complete confidence that we'll have a winning season.

God Is Our Defense 46:1-7

The psalm begins with a summary of the team: "God is our refuge and strength [our defense and our offense], a very present help in trouble. Therefore we will not fear" (46:1-2). The psalmist is in a whole lot of trouble and has plenty of reason to fear. His opponent has sent its three fiercest players onto the field at the same time: earthquake, hurricane, and volcano (46:2-3). So how can the psalmist say, "We will not fear"? Is that just sports psychology talking?

No, this is faith in God talking. In the middle of this malevolent and malicious maelstrom, the writer is completely calm: "There is a river whose streams make glad the city of God, the holy habitation of the Most High" (46:4). He's found a beautiful stream of refreshing comfort—God's presence.

Whatever the other team throws at us, whomever they bring on the field, our star player, our team of one, is on our side: "God is in the midst of her; she shall not be moved; God will help her when morning dawns. The nations rage, the kingdoms totter; he utters his voice, the earth melts. The Lord of hosts is with us; the God of Jacob is our fortress" (46:5–7).

When God's on our side, we don't fear the other side.

"So, are we just on defense all the time?"
God is our offense as well, and gets us a win.

God Is Our Offense 46:8–11

Having defended his people on the one-yard line, God then turns defense into offense, takes it to the house, and routs the opposition. We just stand and watch: "Come, behold the works of the Lord, how he has brought desolations on the earth. He makes wars cease to the end of the earth; he breaks the bow and shatters the spear; he burns the chariots with fire" (46:8–9).

But can I not play too? Can I at least do some blocking? Nope. God says, "Be still, and know that I am God. I will be exalted among the nations, I will be exalted in the earth!" (46:10). Just sit and watch, God says. This is a team of one. Now that's a special team! Just be glad we're on his side and he's on ours. "The Lord of hosts is with us; the God of Jacob is our fortress" (46:11).

This team of one means one team always wins.

Changing Our Story with God's Story

In the greatest victory ever won, Jesus appeared on the field two thousand years ago when his team was down-and-out. His historic defense and offense not only resisted the enemy's attacks but routed him with a resurrection when it looked like all was lost. He's on our side. He is our side. He's our defense and offense. He's our team of one.

Summary: What can give me confidence in the future victory of the church? *Be still and watch God win for you at the cross of Christ.*

Question: How can you get better at being still and knowing God?

Prayer: Victorious God, thank you for defending me and defeating my enemies at the cross. Continue your victory in your church and in my life as I put my trust in you.

God's fans should be louder than sports fans.

47

Make More Noise!

PSALM 47

According to *Guinness World Records*, the Kansas City Chiefs Arrowhead Stadium is the loudest stadium in the world. On September 29, 2014, Guinness measured an ear-splitting 142.2 dBA, the estimated sound level on a busy aircraft carrier.

Why do sports fans shout, cheer, and clap for their team? It's to inspire the players to win, isn't it? We believe that our hands and our mouths can inject energy and endurance into our team and fuel another victory. Our volume helps their victory.

How can we make more spiritual noise with the result of more spiritual victories? Psalm 47 tells us that God has chosen to connect the volume of our praises with the victories of his power.

We Shout with Joyful Songs 47:1-4

We turn up the volume with our hands and our mouths: "Clap your hands, all peoples!" (47:1). That might not be the favorite verse of Presbyterians like myself. But why not? We clap for athletes, singers, actors, presidents, and many others. Why not for God? He's done more clapworthy things than anyone else.

"Shout to God with loud songs of joy!" (47:1). "Make more noise!" the psalmist says. Turn up the volume. Fill your lungs and let rip. And why not? Does my God not deserve more volume than my team?

We might think that all this noise doesn't sound very dignified, but God doesn't seem to mind. Indeed, he gives us multiple reasons to make maximum noise: "For the LORD, the Most High, is to be feared, a great king over all the earth. He subdued peoples under us, and nations under our feet" (47:2–3). If we really understood all that God has done and is doing for us, we would need ear protection in church.

God's fans should be louder than sports fans.

"But does God really like noise?"
Yes, and he adds to it.

God Shouts with Triumphant Trumpets 47:5–9

God joins in the noise: "God has gone up with a shout, the LORD with the sound of a trumpet" (47:5). God responds to our noise with louder noise. The noisier we get, the noisier God gets. Our volume influences God's victories. Of course, God is not limited by our sound levels, but, usually, he chooses to set the level of his power at the level of our praises. If we increase the volume of our praise, we increase the power of God's victories. God has linked these two speakers together.

No wonder the psalmist urges: "Sing praises to God, sing praises! Sing praises to our King, sing praises! For God is the King of all the earth; sing praises with a psalm!" (47:6–7). "Sing praises" five times. And again, it's not mindless and meaningless singing and shouting. We're given great reasons for great roars: "God reigns over the nations; God sits on his holy throne. The princes of the peoples gather as the people of the God of Abraham. For the shields of the earth belong to God; he is highly exalted!" (47:8–9).

The louder our volume, the larger God's victories.

Changing Our Story with God's Story

This psalm sings about one of God's great victories, and it sings for more of them. That's why, historically, the church often sang this psalm on ascension day. "God has gone up with a shout, the Lord with the sound of a trumpet" (47:5). As Christ ascended in triumph to his throne, he shouted, the angels shouted, the saints in heaven shouted—and the church on earth is called to add to those shouts. We have even greater victories to celebrate than the Old Testament church, and therefore our praises should be all the louder.

Summary: How can we make more spiritual noise to result in more spiritual victories? *We can increase the volume of our praise to increase the victories of God's power.*

Question: How can you increase the volume of your praises and therefore the number of God's victories?

Prayer: Praiseworthy God, help me to make more spiritual noise so that I can see more spiritual victories.

The church isn't finished. The church is forever.

48

Rebranding
the Church

PSALM 48

If you were to ask people to describe the church in three words, what words would top the poll? Here's my guess: *divided, dying, judgmental*. That's a public relations disaster, isn't it? With such a poor public image, no wonder it's so hard to get people interested in coming to church. Many who grew up in the church eventually leave it because they're ashamed of being associated with such a "brand." Even those who stay are sometimes embarrassed about being part of it.

Can we rebrand the church, and, if so, how? In Psalm 48, God rebrands the church. He doesn't do anything innovative, but simply supplies his three words for the church: *beautiful, forever,* and *loved*.

The Church Is Beautiful 48:1–3

The Old Testament church was headquartered on Mount Zion in the city of Jerusalem. The New Testament church started in Jerusalem. God used the language of Mount Zion and Jerusalem to describe the church in heaven (Heb. 12:22). And God used the same language to describe his church in Psalm 48.

What's happening in the church? Listen: "Great is the LORD and greatly to be praised in the city of our God! His holy mountain" (48:1). God is being praised there like nowhere else. That's why it's described as "beautiful in elevation . . . the joy of all the earth, Mount Zion, in the far north, the city of the great King" (48:2). Regardless of how big or small the church is, God hears psalms, hymns, and spiritual songs and says, "Beautiful!" It's so attractive to him that he comes to dwell: "Within her citadels God has made himself known as a fortress" (48:3).

If the church is beautiful, why are we bashful?

"Yes, the church was beautiful in the past, but now it seems as if it's dying." No matter how things might look, the church will never die.

The Church Is Forever 48:4–8

At various points in history, it has looked as though the church were finished. But God stepped in, destroyed her destroyers, and resuscitated the church: "For behold, the kings assembled; they came on together. As soon as they saw it, they were astounded; they were in panic; they took to flight" (48:4–5). God terrified them and trashed them. They chanted, "Finished!" but God chanted, "Forever." "As we have heard, so have we seen in the city of the LORD of hosts, in the city of our God, which God will establish forever" (48:8).

The church isn't finished. The church is forever.

"But no one likes the church."
God does.

The Church Is Loved 48:9–11

The church is amazed by God's love for her: "We have thought on your steadfast love, O God, in the midst of your temple" (48:9). We love to love God's love. We leave a hateful world behind, close the doors, sit down, luxuriate in the love of God, and praise God with joyful songs about his love for his people and his judgments on his enemies: "Let Mount Zion be glad! Let the daughters of Judah rejoice because of your judgments!" (48:11).

Because God loves the church, let us love the church.

Changing Our Story with God's Story

As we let God's words sink in—*beautiful, forever*, and *loved*—we see the church differently, lose our fearful shame, and grow in joyful confidence: "Walk about Zion, go around her, number her towers, consider well her ramparts, go through her citadels, that you may tell the next generation that this is God, our God forever and ever. He will guide us forever" (48:12–14).

Summary: Can we rebrand the church, and, if so, how? *Wear God's brand with confidence and joy.*

Question: How can you publicize God's brand of confidence and joy?

Prayer: Head of the Church, thank you for the church and for making each one in it feel beautiful, established forever, and loved.

If we live for spotlights and flashing lights, we'll die in darkness and disgrace.

49

The Richest Man in the Grave

PSALM 49

Who's the richest person in the world? This question fascinates people. Why so much interest? People like to imagine the kind of life that extreme wealth would give them. The old weekly TV series *Lifestyles of the Rich and Famous* tapped into this fantasy. Now we can access daily updates on massively popular social media accounts like Rich Kids of Instagram and the Kardashian reality show. They all invite us to imagine, "What would my life be like if I were that rich?"

Psalm 49 blows up such fantasies and shows us the reality about riches. *What are the benefits and drawbacks of riches?* God really wants us to hear his answer: "Hear this, all peoples! Give ear, all inhabitants of the world, both low and high, rich and poor together! My mouth shall speak wisdom" (49:1–3). Does he have your attention? Then hear what God has to say about the reality of riches.

Riches Cannot Ransom Us from Death 49:5–9

David described the lifestyle of the rich and famous: full of sin, full of cheating, and full of themselves (49:5–6). Some things never change. Now observe their style of death: "Truly no man can ransom another, or give to God the price of his life, for the ransom of their life is costly and can never suffice, that he should live on forever and never see the pit" (49:7–9). However they might have lived, they always die. Even if they gave all their billions to God, they could never buy one more second of life.

A rich lifestyle has a poor deathstyle.

"Riches cannot stop death, but can they help us in death?"
Riches are helpless and leave us helpless.

Riches Cannot Go with Us in Death 49:10–12, 17

"How much did he leave behind?" journalists ask when the rich die. "Everything!" the psalmist answers. "Even the wise die; the fool and the stupid alike must perish and leave their wealth to others" (49:10). Or, as he reminds us again later, "When he dies he will carry nothing away; his glory will not go down after him" (49:17).

They had a beautiful home for a few years, but now "their graves are their homes forever, their dwelling places to all generations" (49:11). They put their names on buildings, but now their name is on a gravestone. They lived in pomp and pride, but now they lie in the dirt like a dead dog (49:12).

Riches can buy a luxury home but not a luxury grave.

"What about after death? Does money count for anything?"
It's helpless and leaves us helpless in death.

Riches Cannot Help after Death 49:13–20

While the unbelieving rich are being eulogized at their funerals, death is shepherding their souls to a homeless hell (49:13–14). As they go down in weakness and humiliation, they look up and see poor people living in power and glory (49:14). Now it's their turn to envy: "How did this happen?" The poor reply God ransomed their souls from the power of death and hell and therefore received them into heavenly glory (49:15). The rich "will never again see light" (49:19).

If we live for spotlights and flashing lights,
we'll die in darkness and disgrace.

Changing Our Story with God's Story

Let's love our Lord Jesus Christ, our ransom, who said, "the Son of Man came not to be served but to serve, and to give his life as a ransom for many" (Matt. 20:28). Jesus paid it all, all to him we owe.

Summary: What are the benefits and drawbacks of riches? *Riches may help us to live a little, but they cannot help us to die at all.*

Question: How can you relate to money better so you can relate to God better?

Prayer: Rich God, in your mercy give me enough financial riches to live, and more than enough spiritual riches to die.

Sync lips and life to see and savor God.

50

Formalist, Fraudster, or Faithful?

PSALM 50

I write this just days after yet another evangelical celebrity has been exposed as a wickedly immoral man. How was he able to dupe so many for so long? The problem is that we can't see into a person's heart; we see only what's on the outside. That's why, in Psalm 50, God calls us into his court to scan our hearts and issue his interim judgment before we face his final judgment (50:1–6). Although everyone might look similar on the outside, God sees three types of hearts. *What kind of heart do you have?*

The Formalist Has No Heart 50:7–15

Formalists are obsessed with outward forms of religion but pay no attention to the inward heart of religion. They multiply meticulous religious services, but, after scanning their hearts, God testifies against them (50:7), rebukes them (50:8), and rejects them (50:9). Why? It wasn't because of their lack of outward religion, but their lack of inward religion. It's not because they offered sacrifice, but because they only offered sacrifice (50:10–13). It's not for giving animals, but for not giving their hearts.

But God still gives opportunity to repent. He calls them to add their hearts to their formalities: "Offer to God a sacrifice of thanksgiving, and perform your vows to the Most High, and call upon me in the day of trouble; I will deliver you, and you shall glorify me" (50:14–15).

Heartless religion is godless religion.

"What other kind of heart does God warn me about?"
The false heart of the fraudster.

The Fraudster Has a False Heart 50:16–22

Some preach God's word but don't practice his word. To them, God says: "What right have you to recite my statutes or take my covenant on your lips? For you hate discipline, and you cast my words behind you" (50:16–17). Fraudsters have God's truth on their lips but are living a lie (50:17–20). They tick the "God box" on Sunday morning but live like the devil the rest of the week.

Because God hasn't judged them yet, they think, "Oh, God's just like us" (50:21). But now God calls them to repentance: "Now I rebuke you and lay the charge before you. Mark this, then, you who forget God, lest I tear you apart, and there be none to deliver!" (50:21–22).

If your lips and lives are not synced, you and God are not synced.

"How can I be sure I'm not a formalist or a fraud?"
Have the thankful heart of the faithful.

The Faithful Have Thankful Hearts 50:5, 23

Having set aside the formalists and the fraudsters, God finds the faithful and says to them, "Gather to me my faithful ones, who made a covenant with me by sacrifice!" (50:5). They didn't just offer sacrifice; they entered into a committed covenant relationship with the Lord. The faithful offer sacrifice but combine it with thanksgiving: "The one who offers thanksgiving as his sacrifice glorifies me" (50:23). Unlike fraudsters, whose lips and lives are out of sync, the faithful's lips and lives align: "To one who orders his way rightly I will show the salvation of God!" (50:23).

Sync lips and life to see and savor God.

Changing Our Story with God's Story

Jesus fulfilled and lived out this psalm by issuing interim judgments. He scanned hearts, warned formalists and fraudsters, and encouraged the faithful. He does the same today through the preaching of his word. Praise God for giving us interim judgments so we can prepare for the final judgment.

Summary: What kind of heart do you have? *Use God's loving interim judgment to replace a formalist or fraudulent heart with a faithful heart so that you are prepared for God's final forever judgment.*

Question: What kind of heart do you have, and how can you develop a more thankful heart?

Prayer: All-Seeing God, you know my heart. Drive out all formality and fraud and give me a faith-filled and faithful heart of gratitude.

TheStoryChanger.life

To keep changing your story with God's Story, visit www.thestory changer.life for the latest news about more StoryChanger devotionals, to sign up for the StoryChanger newsletter, and to subscribe to the *The StoryChanger* podcast.

Also Available in the StoryChanger Devotional Series

For more information, visit **crossway.org**.